Praise for
Powered by Change

"In the modern world change is the only constant, but few companies and leaders have any clue how to deal with this reality. This book gives them more than a clue. It gives them an entire route map."
Mike Butcher MBE, Editor at Large, TechCrunch

"Jonathan is one of the smartest and most knowledgeable experts on technology, business strategy, and, importantly, the changes which are happening across every aspect of human society. His passion, expertise, and ability to take complex issues around change and simplify them into a profound piece of advice is unparalleled. Embracing change is one of the greatest strengths you can have in today's crazy world, so stop what you're doing and start reading it now!"
Craig Hepburn, Global VP Digital Transformation, Tata Communications

"Jonathan brilliantly captures the essence of change and our changing business landscape; leaving us all talking about building windmills!"
Linda Johnson, Chairman Guernsey Branch, Institute of Directors

"*Powered by Change* is that rare thing. A business book that does something other than take one idea and rework it ad infinitum. Not only is the book stacked with compelling and original insight, there is practical advice on how to put the insight into practice in both a professional and personal context. It's a wonderful book that should stay close to the side of anyone who wants to be a rare thing themselves; someone embracing the furious pace of change in the world and putting it to work for advantage."
Geoff Morley, Global Sales & Marketing Director, Nexo

"Jonathan MacDonald is brilliant. I highly recommend his strategies to any organization that wants to achieve 'long-term' success in today's fast changing business world. I'm a firm believer in making learning fun, and am impressed with how masterfully Jonathan weaves humorous stories together with practical examples to generate thought provoking ideas and unique insights."
US Memory Champion, Chester Santos, author of *Instant Memory Training for Success*

"I have worked with Jonathan on a number of projects over the last few years. These have ranged from working with small teams to challenge their mindset of change through to global regional leaders taking on the headwinds of business change. Every time his tailored, thought provoking, and dynamic approach never fails to create a positive impact. He certainly knows his stuff and always inspires me to build windmills . . ."
Sally Hayes, Engagement & Live Event Specialist

Powered by Change

*How to design your business
for perpetual success*

JONATHAN MACDONALD

NICHOLAS BREALEY
PUBLISHING

London • Boston

First published in 2018 by Nicholas Brealey Publishing
An imprint of John Murray Press
An Hachette UK Company

1

Design by Craig Burgess

Illustrations by Dave Birss

A CIP catalogue record for this title is available from the British Library

Hardback ISBN 978-1-473-66558-3
Trade paperback ISBN 978-1-473-66598-9
Ebook ISBN UK 978-1-473-66600-9
Ebook ISBN US 978-1-473-66934-5

Typeset in Celeste by Hewer Text UK Ltd, Edinburgh
Printed and bound by Clays Ltd, St Ives plc

Nicholas Brealey policy is to use papers that are natural, renewable and
recyclable products and made from wood grown in sustainable forests.
The logging and manufacturing processes are expected to conform
to the environmental regulations of the country of origin.

Nicholas Brealey Publishing
John Murray Press
Carmelite House
50 Victoria Embankment
London EC4Y 0DZ
Tel: 020 3122 6000

Nicholas Brealey Publishing
Hachette Book Group
Market Place Center, 53 State Street
Boston, MA 02109, USA
Tel: (617) 263 1834

www.nicholasbrealey.com
www.jonathanmacdonald.com

Contents

About the Author

Image by dantaylorphotography.com

Jonathan is an inventor, investor, business strategist, and internationally acclaimed speaker. As one of the world's most in-demand thought leaders, he is trusted by the senior executives of well-known global companies including Google, Microsoft, Apple, P&G, Unilever, Nestlé, Lego, Heineken, and IKEA to translate the benefits of perpetual change into invaluable business insight and personal success. Jonathan is a contributor to numerous publications including Google's Think Insights, *Forbes*, and the *British Airways Business Life* magazine. He is the founder of the Thought Expansion Network (http://ten.io), Chief Strategy Officer of Moneycatcha Pty Ltd (http://mcatcha.com), and involved in a number of exciting projects that are proudly powered by change. To book Jonathan to speak at your event please contact Miriam Staley at ms@ten.io, or for more details about his latest activities please visit: http://jonathanmacdonald.com.

Foreword

"What I have to say is most likely not relevant for you. And you have a lot of time," announces Jonathan MacDonald with the ambiguity of English irony.

The stage is set. The large, confident crowd is buzzing with anticipation. High expectations. Lights on. Enter Jonathan MacDonald. Eyes gleaming with an intensive glow. Mad curly hair. A smile that is hard to read, indicating that the fun is about to begin.

After a highly impactful start to his keynote speech delivering many examples of how big, well-established, never-can-die companies had to humble themselves and close shop in the face of the new kids on the block, Jonathan reminds us again, "This is unlikely to be relevant for you. And you have a lot of time."

Now, however, the sense of comfort is evaporating quickly.

Then we are off into a session of deep insights on the art and power of disruptiveness, delivered fast and furiously yet balanced with a contagious and ever-present sense of humor. For the grand finale, Jonathan delivers a section called "this-is-how-I-would-disrupt-you." Scary. He pauses and then gives the following conclusion: "This was probably not relevant for you. And you have a lot of time."

Lights out. The end. Or . . . a new beginning?

Our company is big. You've probably heard of it! It's built from a commitment to our vision—our purpose—*to create a better everyday life for the many people.* There's just an incredible power in the word "better." Whether good or bad, things can always get better. "Better" inspires movement. There is a tremendous dullness and risk in the word "best." Best is so often the beginning of the end. That's why the minute after celebrating an achievement we like to turn to the question: "What could we do much better next time?" This vision aspires to both make things happen today and requires the courage to build ever so slowly for big things tomorrow.

Our company was to become one of the unique business models of the last century built from the ground by Ingvar Kamprad, one of the great entrepreneurs of our time. The recipe consists of a meaningful vision, a crystal-clear but hard-to-achieve business idea, an integrated value chain, and a set of humanistic values that, even if sprung from the deep forests of southern Sweden, have an appeal that travels well. Perhaps most important of all, at its heart is a group of highly motivated, optimistic entrepreneurs with a deliberately naïve approach to everything. Built to last forever.

Or, at least, so we thought.

The world is changing in an exponential way. Urbanization, demographics, and politics move fast and often in unpredictable ways. Digital technologies are changing everything. Any successful 1900s business model will be disrupted either by yesterday's leader or by tomorrow's disruptive novelty.

Make your calls for innovation, and make them fast. Verify what's relevant in your legacy and strengthen it. Refresh your business model. Then pursue exploration. Test and try. Iterate strategy along the way. Enjoy the ride. Maybe it will take you to the next big thing. Maybe not. But you have to try.

I am very grateful for the part Jonathan played in moving us into a new phase of entrepreneurship, using the methods you now have the opportunity to learn on your journey through this book. His insights have been a trigger for us to move, and move faster. I am continually fascinated by his capability to transform and adapt his assistance to what is needed.

He first played the role of the mean provocateur, pushing us from the comfort of denial, out into the fogginess of uncertainty. As our willingness grew and we embarked on a new journey of innovation, we eagerly invited Jonathan to add to the solutions, and he brought forward a set of frameworks to enable us to be powered by change. We then got to know him as a capable yet humble coach, and a knowledgeable expert. In our sessions, Jonathan asked the right questions and led us to uncover the answers. Based on his rich experience, we could pick our benchmarks, tools, and inspirations from what other brilliant people and companies have previously experienced and made work using his methodologies.

Jonathan's advice has always been delivered with respect for our heritage and culture, and with the continual insistence that it has to be us who make the choices. Over time, Jonathan has reminded us of the classic traps that many corporations, of all sizes, have fallen into that have prevented their future growth or prosperity. Traps like a lack of long-term commitment, the fear of stepping outside comfort zones, and the defensive reaction to bending rules. Like the instinct to say no to the unknown, the risk of asking the wrong questions, and even the risk of asking the right questions but at the wrong time. But the most crippling trap is a lack of understanding of how to structure and lead innovation using the necessary tools.

Just as he did for us, within these pages Jonathan has provided the necessary solutions, remedies, and tools for future freedom and success.

After a period of intensive investigation, field trips, and hours of strategizing, we signed off our plans for the next phase of our glorious future. I simply could not resist the temptation to let

Jonathan review them. We met in a crowded downtown London café for what became a couple of hours' reviewing, calibrating, amplifying, and verifying. At this point, Jonathan played the role of an inspired co-driver. When reflecting on our journey together, I appreciate having met a person who so consciously moves from denial-provoking entertainment, to coaching and co-creating. He masters innovation and is passionately fascinated by its forces.

We have just taken the first steps on our new journey. Disruptive innovation still presents a risk, but much more so an opportunity that we find ever so exciting. We are getting better at disrupting our own business. We have learned that we do not lack ideas or spirit. For us, being inspired to put in place new structures, processes, financing, and governance for how to lead innovation has been essential. It might sound boring but ideas will not fly in a big context unless you give them the structure to do so. We have learned to release lots of ideas in exploration through a broad, curious, and non-judgmental approach. We have learned how to turn those ideas into capabilities and then solutions. We are learning the hard way how to embed innovation into our business—in this phase there are no easy tricks; just leadership, purpose, and involvement. We have been challenged to explore new and exciting ways to co-create with other companies, inventors, universities, start-ups, accelerators, and people who just have a great idea. We celebrate our breakthroughs but, to be honest, ditch many bad ideas along the way and write off a bigger number of failures than ever before. Yet still, at the core, are our people and talent who share the same vision and values.

As a highly demanded professional speaker, Jonathan often shares his story generously on stages around the world; moments like his joy and excitement of being appointed as the youngest-ever chairman of the British Music Industries Association at the exact time when file-sharing was disrupting and eventually reshaping that entire industry. In that situation, as in many others that he has experienced throughout his life and career when the unbelievable and unforeseeable happened and happened fast, he had to make the choice between using change as a powering mechanism or viewing it as an enemy. Even today, that choice continues to determine his success or failure—and that of every single company that he has ever come into contact with.

Jonathan carries the evidence and scars of ongoing change and disruption, which simply add to the credibility and power of his message. And it is a message that is now in print.

I am happy to welcome you to the pages you have ahead of you. I can assure you that you are about to be taken on a roller-coaster ride of examples, irony, insight, theories, and a practical toolkit for how to be truly powered by change. I believe that within just a few pages you will agree with me that, unlike so many theoretically interesting but unpractical volumes of management literature, Jonathan's book is actually very useful. Open your mind to the unthinkable. Explore the what-ifs. Allow yourself to dream and ideate. Test your thinking about how you would disrupt your own business—because somebody out there is already working hard on it.

It's highly unlikely, but if nothing has really moved you by the time you get to the final chapter, then you can always conclude:

"This is not relevant for me. And I have plenty of time."

Jesper Brodin,
Chief Executive, IKEA Group

PART 1

The Windmill Theory

CHAPTER ONE

The Reality of Perpetual Change

There's an ancient proverb that states: "When the winds of change are blowing, some build a wall; others build a windmill." It's a saying that's thousands of years old, but it could not be more relevant to what's happening all around us today.

Life and business, people and politics, economics and technology—all facets of our twenty-first-century capitalist existence—are constantly changing. How we respond will determine our survival or failure as individuals, as companies, and as a society at large. In a transient business environment where consultants McKinsey & Company estimate that only one-third of transformation strategies actually succeed, it has never been harder to see accurately what's happening around us, interpret that information efficiently, and develop effective strategies that are executed in a successful way. This book is designed to help do just that, because the alternative is bleak. Quite simply, more than half the top businesses of today are unlikely to survive.

Why is this so? After all, commentators have been warning for some time about new paradigms, the need for business agility, and how only those truly agile and adaptive companies will survive. Despite that, we have already seen in this young century the decline—and in some cases demise—of names from Yahoo! to Nokia to BlackBerry to Kodak. Each spent billions of dollars on brand-building, senior executive teams with great track records, and costly external advisers—yet still fell foul of those inevitable winds of change.

Much has been written about what unites these failures and what lessons their falls from grace contain. Yet such analysis simply reinforces the fallacy that the inability to adapt to change is something that only a mere handful of businesses are guilty of.

In fact, the very opposite is true. Despite the colossal size and reputations of the world's largest corporations, only a few are going to survive the changes that are to batter their business models and strategies over the next 50 years. There are three reasons for this.

1. A greater degree of change is on the way than has occurred in the past.

2. The rate of ongoing change is going to be a lot faster than we have previously experienced.

3. History shows that companies are poor at coping with and responding effectively to change.

Consider this: *88% of the companies that were in the Fortune 500 list of the world's largest corporations in 1965 are not in that list today.* Over an even shorter sample period of time, corporate resilience is not much better, with *74% of the Fortune 100 list having disappeared since 1980.*[1]

The reason we are so bad at adapting to change is that we constantly misunderstand the nature and speed of such change. Change is seen as a threat, so our mindset focuses on strategies to react and adapt to it rapidly, with the aim of protecting what we have at all costs. In reality, the rate of change is quickening so rapidly that I confidently predict that in the future, the 88% statistic I quoted will apply to a timeframe of just five years, rather than the 50-year period of the past.

I truly believe that this is a monumental problem facing all companies, but our businesses are either choosing to ignore it altogether or are tackling it with fundamentally the wrong approach. Businesses should be learning to anticipate change, they could be setting the agendas rather than merely following them, and above all they must be committed to genuinely innovating, rather than copying. As our record in clairvoyance and fortune-telling leaves much to be desired, this requires a complete reappraisal of how humankind is wired to view and respond to change, as well as an acknowledgment that throughout history the mere presence of change has actually been the only constant.

"Change is the only constant."

It's hard to argue against that statement looking through the rear-view mirror, isn't it? So why do we as humans, entrepreneurs, and leaders have such a problem with organizing ourselves not in a three-year program of change, a five-year plan, or even a ten-year vision, but in readiness for always-happening, never-stopping perpetual change?

The answer has much to do with the fact that change doesn't happen at a uniform rate but in an exponential fashion. As every day goes past—since the Big Bang or any other dawn of time of your choice—the pace of change each day has gotten faster. Consider the way that nature is structured in evolutionary terms; with one cell dividing into two, that duo becoming four, that quartet turning into eight, and eight cells doubling to sixteen. A 16-fold growth just four steps after there was only one cell.

Nothing naturally happens in a perfectly linear way, and in fact, the way that change accelerates and is organic is something that we have been programmed as humans to want to resist.

This resistance is our natural comfort zone because we like feeling in control of our situation, even if the evidence would suggest that the reality is that we never truly are. It's a worrying trait of humankind, in our careers, and in business, because comfort is something that, despite feeling good at the time, means we are decoupled from the true rate of change. As it is so popular to resist the winds of change, the question then becomes whether that is perhaps a valid decision to take. I personally don't believe that it is, if the desire to create and build future success exists. The way to really view the future when we look at the contexts of modern business, society, and technology is an acknowledgment and acceptance of the fact that today is actually the slowest pace of change we will ever experience.

The change in the next 10 years in terms of technical development, computerization, and all other associated capabilities is likely to be the same as the entire set of such changes over the last 50 years.

Change is exponential and change accelerates.

The mere thought of that may make our minds and bodies groan, limited as they are by a linear timeframe. It may seem like a huge exaggeration to envisage transformation five times greater or faster than the progress of the last half-century: the invention of fiber optics, e-mail, IVF, barcodes, the internet, the World Wide Web, mobile phones, and a deluge of digitally connected devices.

Yet our current reality is that we're already at a time where the average smartphone has the same computing power as the whole of NASA did in 1969.[2] Our minds simply cannot conceive of what 2026 will be like if the rate of such change increases exponentially. All the evidence suggests though that this is exactly what will happen, and therefore there is no historical, present, or future validity in deciding to resist change.

With resistance futile, survival—and indeed the potential for us and our businesses to truly thrive—will rely on us moving from a mindset of one-off change management to one of how we manage the perpetual change that is accelerating across trends, industries, macroeconomic forces, societies, behaviors, and markets. This change comes in many forms, from globalization to the explosive growth in artificial intelligence and robotics technology. It incorporates geopolitical upheaval, such as the emergence of China as one of the world's leading economies, and also includes environmental and societal challenges including climate change and sustainability. Then there are aging demographics, talent and skills shortages, changing terrorism threats, and the exponentially growing danger that every business potentially faces from cybercrime. These are changes that affect businesses small to large but there will be others pertaining to different segments, from tax changes for start-ups to different inheritance provisions for family firms. This is the business world we operate within. It's not just about a new technology; it's about every single factor in the external landscape that impacts on every part of an organization internally.

Everything that we know and have known is changing faster, and it is the ability to respond to these changes that determines our future and our success.

Walls or windmills?

Perpetual change is our reality, but it would seem that the business reaction is usually one of inaction. Businesses are inured to being told they are living and operating in an era of constant change. They want a break from corporate transition programs; they think they have much more time than they do. They are tired of change and ideally seem to want an easy period in which to make hay while the sun shines now.

I hold a very strong belief that the ability of an organization, group of people, or individual to survive and thrive in a world of perpetual change depends on whether they are building a windmill to use the winds of change as a powering mechanism, or erecting a wall in an attempt to resist the forces they face.

This is more often than not a legacy issue. It is critical that CEOs and leaders initiate transformations in culture that make their organizations more change-responsive—even if they will no longer be around to see the continued fruit of their work. Too often I have come across business leaders and company executives who are simply riding out the last few years of their pre-retirement tenure or before they move on, hoping against hope that they will be out of the door before the onslaught of change demolishes everything that they have presided over. Sadly, they often don't seem to care that by doing this they are betting against the entire potential future of their company or brand, and are exchanging a few years of personal comfort for the long-term pain of those who try to follow the path they have laid down.

That is why it is so important to have the mindset, understanding, and tools that allow us, and our success, to be truly powered by change. Because that's the only future that exists.

This is not just another business book warning about the inevitability of change; it is a definitive survival handbook. In reading it, you have a choice. You can throw it to one side and think you already know the answers and that you're doing everything you need to survive. Or you can read on and learn how to grow your business hugely. You can understand what it would take to retain your best members of staff and find ways that you can continually release products and services that change the market. You can decide that you want to be able to sleep at night knowing that you are doing something that actually, really, truly matters. Then you can build on the lessons shared and heed the warnings of those who failed last time around. You can develop into a leader who can future-proof your business—not because you reject and repel change but because you accept its inevitability and embrace the new and exciting journeys that it can take you on.

Are you going to build a wall, or find out how to build a wind-mill? The choice is yours.

CHAPTER TWO

Powered by Change:
A Personal Story

I am Jonathan MacDonald, and the story of my childhood is best described by these two pictures. The one on the left was taken eight weeks before I started school. I was four years old, an innocent boy, with bright, inquisitive eyes as yet untethered and undamaged by life. Life was just about playing. The second picture is taken exactly one year later. I had 11 stitches on my

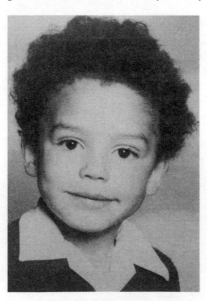 

right cheek, a stab wound in my left hand, and the lead from an assault with a pencil still embedded in my right hand. My eyes in this second picture tell the story. The innocence was gone. Life sucked. I was supposed to be out playing with my friends but I was already experiencing some of life's limitations.

On my first day at school, I was noticed at once for my frizzy hair, taken aside by two schoolkids in my lunch break, and stabbed in the hand with a pencil. The lead remains in my hand to this day. I had been given up at birth by my natural parents, put into foster care, and then adopted some time later. My adoptive parents noticed a change in me from this very first day of school. Sadly, this assault was only the beginning of 11 years of mental and physical abuse. In this period, I had numerous bones in my body broken. My nose was fractured so many times that there is no cartilage remaining in it now. And I have a big bump at the back of my skull where my head was rammed into a red plastic fire bell when I was aged seven. Upon reflection, it's hard to tell whether I asked for help enough to warrant it, but nonetheless, nobody intervened or stopped this abuse.

At the age of five, I was in charge of me and had to decide how I wanted to be treated, whether I wanted to survive, and what to do in order to ensure that happened. My answer to this quandary on that first day at school was to hide under a chair in the reception area. Teachers coaxed me out and asked my parents to collect me. My first question to them was whether every day at school was going to be like this. I was instructed that I had to go to school, and in my eyes, this gave me little choice. I had to somehow deal with it. Over the next 11 years, the shapes and forms that this abuse took progressed and mutated, but this was also a time of enormous learning for me, not in the educational disciplines I was at school to master but in the art of survival. I did not realize that the lessons I learned here were going to power my future, but that's exactly what happened. The changes that I went through in my schooldays powered what happened to me in the rest of my life.

I did some early analysis at the age of six. There were three children of color in my school in leafy Surrey, in the heart of the south of England. Julian and David were my friends, but Julian was the fastest runner in the school. He was also a target for bullies, but nobody could catch him quick enough to bully him. And David was a talented football player, which got him off the hook too. I had no running ability and no football prowess; I was firmly in the sights of the bullies and I couldn't get away. It was at this point that I realized that life is unfairly weighted and that nobody else apart from me was going to address that unfairness. But what was I to do, targeted, highly vulnerable, and pretty defenseless?

I never accepted that being a victim was the best outcome. I deemed it less optimal than simply surviving. I also realized during this time that I had one redeeming quality: I could articulate my speech and express myself in meaningful ways. I tested this ability when I had the chance to speak directly to my tormentors. I worked hard on this ability, and by the time I was eight I was able to converse with them for three and a half minutes before they started attacking me. What I said clearly resonated somewhat with them, because they would apologize for what they were about to do. But it didn't stop them beating the hell out of me. That was progress of a sort but I needed other diversion tactics.

When I was eight, I ran into a school hallway and ended up by accident in the middle of an audition for parts in *Nero*, a play about the Roman emperor of that name. I saw my opportunity to hide. I had never read the script and did not know the plot, but realized that while I was on the stage, nobody could physically get to me or hurt me. Stumped for something to say, I admitted that I knew little about Nero but that my world was on fire too and I needed protection to survive. I got the key part, and from that moment onward I auditioned for every play that my school produced, because nobody could bully me on the stage. The stage became my safe place. I knew now that every-body was not on my side but I had an escape from the torment. I was able to be on stage while simultaneously changing the way that people thought about me, and it was the happiest I had ever been in my life.

It didn't stop the bullying, of course. Nothing I did seemed to be able to stop it, and I seeped into a mindset that this was what my life was always going to be like and I couldn't do much about it. It is a human reality that we cannot help but predict our future based on our past. It doesn't matter how illogical that is. When things go wrong enough, people feel that they are pre-constructed victims and that their place in life is to suffer. It is extraordinarily hard to break out of that mindset, and that's where I was for 11 years. The happiness that I thought I had found soon dissipated. I was on a downward spiral and things just seemed to get worse and worse before they got better.

The last day that I was bullied in school was when I was 16 years old. I was stabbed in the stomach with a barbecue fork.

The boy who did this had been a key tormentor for the past four years of my secondary school education, and I had been warned that day before the attack that I would be traveling home in an ambulance. That would have certainly been unusual; most of my beatings had stopped just short of necessitating that emer-gency call. I was used to the thud of baseball bats on my kneecaps and air being sucked from my lungs when I was kicked in the stomach. But on that day, this particularly vicious bully had a plan for something much worse. In that moment while I was lying on the floor, skewered by the barbecue fork, I suddenly saw the decision between being a victim and being a survivor with a

13

clarity I had not experienced before. I decided at that moment that not only was I not going to let this attack beat me, I was also never again going to be physically abused.

To construct a thought that something is not going to be allowed to happen again means that one has to take the learnings from the past and turn them on their head. Lying on the floor, I came to the instant realization that my survival was down to myself. I was being bullied because I was allowing myself to be a victim. I had the ability to take control and prevent this from happening again. Until then, I had always rationalized the bullying as something that happened to me, rather than anything I could do something about. Lying on the ground, I realized that I had to use the constant, unexpected change that always seemed to come my way as something that could help me grow and develop, rather than something that I just repelled and hoped against hope would eventually go away.

I believe that what happened in my brain that day was an empowering mechanism that used a particularly unpleasant circumstance to take back control. My previous failings would no longer be seen as negative outcomes but lessons that I could learn from. The reason that I went on to live free of bullying is because I learned how I was allowing it to happen and made the choices to ensure that it never happened again. I realized that I was inadvertently giving permission for the bullying to happen. This was not about forgiving my bullies; it was about accepting accountability for events that were going wrong and devising strategies to correct and change those situations.

What did I do differently? I recognized that I was allowing myself to be bullied by continuing the behavior that my bullies had learned to anticipate.

I always walked home from school the same way, and 50% of the attacks happened on my journey home. So I changed my route.

I had often wondered why my friends had never stood up for me or prevented the attacks. Later, it turned out that they had actually been complicit with the bullies, allowing me to be victimized so that my tormentors left them alone. I changed my friends.

And the third, proactive, action that I took was to learn judo and kickboxing so that I could protect myself by knowing how to use my bullies' force and strength against them. I figured that I only needed to stand up to a bully once and win, and the bullying would stop. I changed my attitude.

I discovered that it is relatively easy to change your mindset once you are willing to believe that your outcomes can change. I also found that it is relatively quick to see the benefits of doing so. It is the *willingness* that is key. I decided on the ground after being stabbed that this situation needed to change, and that I needed to be the agent of that change; realizing which parts of the picture I could adjust by altering my own behaviors and personal outlook.

This was a pivotal point in my development, and I would love to be able to say that everything has been linear, straightforward, and on an upward trajectory since then. However, that is rarely how life works, and a decade or so later I found myself driving down the motorway knowing that my business, life, and financial prospects were apparently in ruin. I was in a state of total despair, contemplating what would happen if I simply jerked the wheel and decided to end it all.

How did this happen? In a different way from the bullying of my school days, I had allowed myself to feel that I was a victim with few choices. After working in my family's gift shop and eschewing my previous ambition to become a barrister, I opened a music retail outlet and moved into the nascent online music scene by setting up Mmusic.com in the late 1990s when there was only one other music retail website in the UK.

The company amassed a dominant share of this new market for a very short period of time, making me very wealthy in my twenties; and I had also begun to believe that everything in my business career would always go exactly to plan. Three years later, I was the youngest-ever chairman of the British Music Industries Association and was persuaded to put a million pounds into a TV channel called The Musician's Channel, which would teach people how to play and sing music on television. I became chief executive, mortgaged my business and property, and put everything into this new company. For a moment in time, we attracted a million viewers per show in a period when MTV was only being watched by around 100,000 people in the UK.

Working with the BMI and politicians, we also succeeded in getting British law changed to enable all state secondary schoolchildren to study music without sacrificing another subject. However, things did not turn out as I had envisaged, as a clause in our legal agreement entitled my business partner in the Musician's Channel to dilute my equity ownership of my stake in the firm, allowing me to be bought out extremely cheaply.

I ended up losing everything I had put into the business except for £12.67. Married with two children aged three and one, I even ended up living for a while behind a pub in a Nissan Micra, which was the only major possession that I didn't have to give back to the bank.

That was when I thought about swerving the steering wheel and crashing out of life. But then I started to think more positively and convinced myself that things could not possibly get worse. I had read the work of psychiatrist and Holocaust survivor Viktor Frankl which explains the gap between stimulus and response, arguing that in that gap lies our growth and our freedom. He was identifying the difference between a reaction that we often have—the re-enactment of something—and the moment in time when we can *choose* how to respond, and truly own the sovereignty of our intellect.

I saw again, just as I had seen at school, that the choice I had was between being a victim or being a survivor. I again chose very clearly and consciously to be a survivor, although I have to say that this time it was a really close call. What made the difference at this point was surprisingly not my children or my upbringing, but a study I had read about patients' deathbed regrets. The regret ranked fifth on that list resonated incredibly strongly with me. That oh-so-common regret is this: "I wish that I had let myself be happier."

I had to be a survivor, I decided, because in spite of all my wealth and achievements, I had never been truly happy.

However, when I returned to my about-to-be-repossessed home, I realized that there had been occasions in my life when I had indeed been very happy. When I condensed those moments to their essence, I could see that these were the moments I had spent on a stage, interacted with inspirational people, and was able to make people see things in a different way and expand their thinking. I had sudden clarity that the combination of those three specific elements made me content. None of those features were particularly going to make me as much money as I had already made and lost. But I saw then that I am essentially driven not by material riches, but by working and living in a way that enables me to do those three things.

Despite that new nugget of truth tucked away at the back of my mind, it wasn't a simple or straightforward future to build. I went on to found a number of unsuccessful companies and work unhappily for several others—but each time learning more, and applying myself to make the necessary changes. It took a while but I eventually decided to only work with people who are willing to expand their thinking, which is how I came to create the Thought Expansion Network (TEN) and develop my professional speaking career.

Suffice it to say that I gained a lot from these experiences. During this time, I also cemented my conviction that most businesses have little chance of survival—regardless of their size—if they do not take action to equip themselves to confront a business world of perpetual change.

My purpose in much of my childhood was simply to survive, and that is what I just about managed to do. But merely surviving change, and circumstance, does not by itself equip us to succeed. I learned that what I was all about was finding solutions, making myself secure, and having a stage on which to operate. I was able to elevate my personal purpose to the extent that I now see the reason for my existence as enabling people to change the way that they think, in order to increase their chances of achieving maximum happiness and success. But I only realized that this is what I am at my core after I discarded all the rubbish that I had tricked myself into believing that I was before that. I realized eventually that what drives me the most is changing the way that people think. But I needed to rid myself of a lot of biases and past beliefs in order to get there. I now realize that the world needs to think differently about change—a fact that motivates me hugely to speak on stages around the globe to as many people as I can.

Practice what you preach

At the time of writing, I am also in my eighth start-up. It is clear to me now that success is a combination of great ideas, brilliant execution, fantastic timing, and recognition of the consequences of actions. It is also about not listening to too many people's ideas, as demonstrated by the well-known image[3] that shows what the iPhone 7 would have looked like if the company had built it in exactly the way that all the users and experts were telling them to. It is safe to say that it certainly does not look like a world-class, desirable piece of technology! For sure, one also needs a little luck in business, but the main conviction I have been left with is that success is extremely unlikely to ever be an accident.

Just as I took control of my various situations and learned not to have a victimized mindset, organizations need to know how to adapt themselves to what our perpetually changing world will throw at them.

I now have a black belt in kickboxing. I have taught myself to be tough, not in physical muscle but in mental agility to avoid conflict. And when conflict does occur, the best force to utilize is the one that is pitched against you, since it is easier to use that force than to generate one's own.

This is true in the world of business too. Organizations can mobilize the forces of change that are raging against them to power their future successes. This is business judo. The disruptive changes that are transforming business and our modern-day landscape contain forces that are too strong and powerful to restrain or fight back against. The only way to deal with unpredictable, perpetually accelerating rates of change is to devise strategies that win—not through our own force but through the power of the very changes that otherwise threaten to overcome us.

From the day that ended my bullying, I believe I have been powered by change. I am now in a position to share those lessons with businesses that face almost certain disaster unless they take major action that will enable them to survive whatever the world has to throw at them over the next decades.

Powered by change

The key is to look at how such businesses can respond, rather than react, to perpetual change and adapt their operations to survive and thrive. I call the strategic thinking that I have developed to help companies do this, and that underpins this entire book, the "Windmill Theory." It is based on the necessity to have four essential blades that work in a cohesive, integrated way in order to harness the winds of change and use them to our advantage. Those blades are ones of purpose, people, product, and process. While on the surface this might sound obvious or even simplistic, let me assure you that putting the specific "Windmill Theory" strategy into action has yielded incredible results for some of the world's largest companies. I am privileged to have assisted organizations like ValueLabs, Unilever, Microsoft, Proctor & Gamble, and IKEA over the years.

When I first went into IKEA and met with Jesper Brodin, who was at that point the chief executive of the company's Swedish operations, the company was, by its later admission, starting to feel fairly comfortable about how it was operating. This was despite some problematic areas of the group, such as its customer service and difficult-to-understand furniture assembly instructions. My critique of the business was brutal. "The biggest danger you face," I told Jesper, "is that you are in danger of not being able to respond to anything because you are so large and successful." Over time, my words have helped boost the company into action and inspired a program that it put together using the four blades of the windmill as the most effective mechanism to respond to perpetual change. This same approach you will find within these pages is what has helped IKEA to totally reposition its agility, responsiveness, and innovation. Jesper has since told me that the only objection he has to the "Windmill Theory" is that I should no longer call it a theory because IKEA has put it into practice and proved that it works. It has also worked for many other companies.

This book is structured to take you through the imperative that change is perpetual and needs to be continually addressed, rather than avoided. The first half of the book explains the reasons for this and looks at some of the ways that companies have responded.

The second half will show you how to construct your own individual business windmill to use the winds of change to drive your company, rather than blow it away. Our windmill design that enables us to thrive in an era of perpetual change has four blades: Purpose, People, Product, and Process. The **Purpose** of a company is what the organization thinks it is for: what it does. The way that its leaders define this function has a direct effect on how fluid and innovative it is when faced with transformative forces. A company's **People** are then key to the successful achievement or adaptation of whatever that purpose is. Do they have the willingness and ability to be flexible and imaginative in what they do? Clarity of purpose and empowered, engaged people then have to be manifested into attractive, useful, and highly marketable **Products** and services. And to do this effectively, a business will need porous and relevant **Processes**.

Building an organization with all four fully functioning blades equips it with the fluidity of thinking, flexible people power, correctly positioned product offerings, and the nimble systems that are needed to cope with the change that is coming along the line.

But first I want to address the general directions of the changes that are evidently going to transform the world as we know it, and give you some tools that will help you know how to go about structuring your responses to them.

CHAPTER THREE

Evolutions and Revolutions

It is abundantly clear where some of the strongest winds of change are blowing. The three gales of *disintermediation, democratization,* and *disruption* have been swirling for some time. But they are coming together in a much more significant tempest that is bringing about an array of changes that promise to totally transform the business world over the coming decade. What recognition exists in your organization of these transformative changes and how they are likely to develop and grow further over the next few years? Think about the following three categories and consider what your business's response is to each.

Disintermediation

The first of our three D-forces is defined in economics as the removal of intermediaries in a supply chain, cutting out middlemen in a series of transactions. This term "disintermediation" was originally applied to the US banking industry, back in the 1960s where customers avoided the third-party services of banks for savings accounts and began investing directly in securities, insurance companies, mutual funds, and shares and bonds. This trend was furthered in the UK by the "Big Bang" changes in Britain's financial markets in 1986, when electronic means superseded face-to-face open outcry trading, and the historic distinction between stock jobbers and brokers was abolished. In the late 1990s the term "disintermediation" became widely popularized as the effect that the first wave of the internet was having on physical sales outlets, with the dramatic shrinkage of video-rental chains, bookshops, and high-street travel-agency branches because consumers could increasingly procure these goods directly from the supplier, or online, without the need for these bricks-and-mortar middlemen.

In the subsequent waves of the internet's development, disintermediation has spread to affect providers of fundamental services such as hotel rooms and city taxi-ride services. Airbnb and Uber now allow customers of these commodities to access whole new areas of supply, directly via the private ownership of other individuals and businesses that were not previously easily available to them. Other companies are applying similar "sharing economy" models to peer-to-peer lending, foreign currency exchange, house-buying, car-sharing, business crowdfunding, and many other sectors. And, while new intermediaries, such as Amazon and eBay, have emerged in a trend that has been called "reintermediation," their futures are evolving rapidly too. In manufacturing and industry, supply chains have been streamlined and made more efficient with just-in-time deliveries and closer relationships between major producers and a smaller elite group of partners.

We are living in an era where the entire marketplace in any industry vertical is being fundamentally disintermediated. That means that whatever value chain you observe (where the term "value chain" includes activities such as logistics, marketing, design, sales, distribution, and so forth), you will see that the parties in the middle, be they brokers, aggregators, or agencies, are decreasingly required on a daily basis. Someone has a space in their car and somebody else wants a lift somewhere; the sharing economy provides the connection between the two and so you remove the taxi firms in the middle, just as Uber does. Somebody has a spare room in their house and someone else wants to stay in that town. Again, the ability to bring the two parties together through a company with the networked power of Airbnb results in a direct transaction to rent that room in the house.

Disintermediation is essentially the closing of the gap between supply and demand. Like many other elements you will find in this book, it is primarily caused by an increase in the affordability and capability of technology. In days gone by, people who had space in their car would have had to create some form of signpost on top of their vehicle to attract attention, or wait and find a hitchhiker. Nowadays, anyone can register to be a driver and once approved, you run the Uber app in your vehicle and anyone nearby who needs a ride can find and track your vehicle easily. Technology has disintermediated the requirement for parties in the middle who used to be there to ensure that the supply was connected to the demand by way of their company or organization. While some see the Uber or Airbnb portals as a form of modern-day intermediary, they could perhaps better be perceived simply as the frictionless mechanism through which the person with the demand connects directly with the person who can supply what they need.

It is a huge mistake, however, to think that disintermediation is something that has largely already happened. Instead, technology is enabling it to take new forms, and no business is immune. Even in our personal lives, intermediaries are being eradicated. The Internet of Things (IoT) is essentially disintermediating direct physical individual involvement in making industrial and domestic appliances function. Factories where sensors allow machines to effectively communicate with others further up and down the manufacturing chain are disintermediating human involvement. At home, if your computer programs when the lights and heating switch on, you no longer have to do this physically when you arrive back to a cold house. Artificial intelligence, which is being called "the fourth industrial revolution," has the potential to take this much, much further, questioning the roles of humans in many functions that will instead be performed perfectly and more efficiently by machines.

Radical disintermediation happens in every single industry vertical where supply and demand exists.

This doesn't need to be a business-to-consumer (B2C) relationship. It can equally be business-to-business (B2B). Disintermediation has neither priority nor preference. Anywhere there is a gap between supply and demand that could be shortened or removed, disintermediation takes hold.

Think about disintermediation in the context of your company or business project:

- What are your current ways of linking what is sold to what is bought?

- If a system were able to shorten those links, how could it work?

- How much more value could be added to both the supply and the demand side?

- If a competitor were to create that system, how would it impact you?

It's worth spending some time on these questions and properly assessing the answers. Even if you're unable to think of an answer, pause and return to the question later. It may be one of the most valuable exercises you do in terms of reducing the risk to you that disintermediation could pose.

Democratization

In politics, democratization has myriad representations, encouraging the rule of the people through freely and fairly elected parliaments and governments, and fostering the growth of democratic institutions such as an accountable judiciary, free education, and open media. In business, however, the change that democratization is bringing concerns the freedom and ability of any part of the value chain to play any other part.

Consumers can be investors through crowdfunding platforms like Kickstarter that enable anyone to fund the launch of a new product or service; they can also be lenders through peer-to-peer companies such as Zopa.com and microfinance sites such as Kiva, as well as foreign currency providers through firms such as TransferWise.

Individuals can also be manufacturers through the maker movement in 3D printing, enabling anyone to create their own goods. And they can also be retailers, with public online marketplaces like eBay or Etsy enabling anyone to sell almost any item. The consumer end of the value chain now has the same computing power as the corporate end, driving intense democratization across any industry vertical.

Radical democratization happens in every single industry vertical where production, distribution, and consumption exist. And, like its political cousin, business democratization is being driven by a number of factors. Higher levels of personal wealth mean that individuals have increased assets that they can seek to share or sell. This is driving growth in social mobility and equality, while technological developments are making such transactions more possible, accessible, and affordable.

Amidst this continuing and fast-evolving change, it is prudent not to consider any stability in today's marketplace as a sign of future stability. As today is the slowest pace of change we will ever experience, the chances of radical democratization will increase tomorrow.

Think about democratization in the context of your company or business project:

- In what ways could it be possible, no matter how feasible in the present day, for your customers or end users to provide or supply what it is that you currently do?

- In what ways could you use this capability for the benefit of your organization, the customers, and end users?

- What are the things that are currently stopping this from happening?

- How long do you feel these barriers to entry will continue?

Disruption

Radical disintermediation and democratization are extraordinarily disruptive and are not necessarily visible as they take hold. Unknown market entrants spring up from everywhere, without fanfare, and redesign the marketplace on the fly. As we explore what it means to be powered by change, you will find a repeated appeal for urgency, the need to act fast and not delay. This is because the rate of radical disintermediation and democratization accelerates; thus, the probability of radical disruption accelerates also.

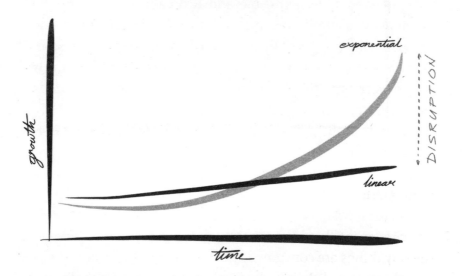

We tend to plan our growth on a linear trajectory. We are inclined to approximate the next five or ten years as a relatively standard progression from where we already are. However, the rate of exponential change speeds up all the time, and it is the gap between the two that presents the probability of radical disruption.

Our requirement to build a windmill increases each day, and thus this handbook that you are now holding in paper or digital form is even more relevant today than it was yesterday, and so forth.

To help us identify radical disruption, we need to look at its characteristics. From my observation, radical disruption tends to follow a similar pattern of events wherever it is found, and is illustrated by this graph:

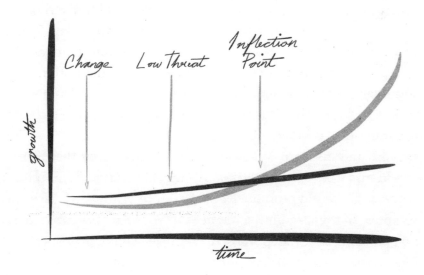

STEP ONE

The first event that tends to happen is a fundamental change in the way things are consumed, the way things are produced, or the way things are distributed. For example, in 2004 the American DVD-rental chain Blockbuster consisted of nearly 60,000 employees in more than 9,000 stores globally. Millions of people daily would visit a Blockbuster store and rent a movie. One of the primary sources of revenue was late return penalties, made possible due to the requirement of physically returning the movie back into a store.

But the rise of the World Wide Web meant that people had already started to adjust the way they bought and experienced entertainment, and with the launch of iTunes in 2001 the transformation in the way that people acquired music really took hold. In the DVD-rental market, it was clear that online formats would not hold the same opportunity for late return penalties. However, despite this very clear wind of change, Blockbuster maintained its wall with all its might.

STEP TWO

The second event that tends to happen is a widespread low threat rating. In 2001, Reed Hastings, founder of Netflix, flew to Dallas to propose a partnership to Blockbuster chief executive Jon Antioco and his team. What Hastings proposed was that Netflix would run the online version of Blockbuster and in return, Blockbuster would promote Netflix in-store. Antioco's board was receptive to the idea until a member of Antioco's executive team pointed out that the proposed changes would probably cost Blockbuster $200m in the loss of charging late fees for physical rentals and another $200m in the branding costs of launching Blockbuster online. Ultimately, the Blockbuster board decided to reject the opportunity and reportedly laughed Hastings out of the office. Hastings returned to Netflix, which continued to develop a service that avoided retail locations, lowered operating costs, and offered its customers far greater variety and choice. Instead of charging to rent videos, it offered rolling subscriptions, which made annoying late fees unnecessary. Customers could watch a video for as long as they wanted or "return" it and get a new one.

At this stage, Blockbuster did what many organizations do; it considered all of these changes that were starting to trickle through the market to be a low threat. They felt that people would take a long time to adjust to a totally new way of renting movies, and they continued to bet on their existing model due to its historic success.

Kodak made exactly the same bet, believing that people would take a long time to want to use a phone as a camera, and until that moment actually came, they thought they could continue to own the camera market as they had done in the past. Equally, when I was chairman of the British Music Industries Association in 2001, we felt it would take a long time for people to switch from buying physical CDs to listening to digital music online. Amazing isn't it, how this mindset was so widespread then, and still prevails today?

STEP THREE

The third event that tends to happen is an inflection of the exponential change into mainstream adoption. People increasingly started to use Netflix and realized it was a more intuitive way of renting movies. Meanwhile, Blockbuster watched the ever-increasing growth and adoption for its competitors' service, but realized that it would have to alter its business model and damage its profitability in order to even begin to compete with Netflix at this point. Blockbuster was trapped. The company's revenues and profit dropped so low that it filed for bankruptcy protection in September 2010. In April 2011, the remaining stores were bought at auction, and by 2016 only 51 stores remained. Now the Blockbuster brand has mostly been retired.

By the time there's an inflection point into mainstream adoption, it's often too late to respond.

Many companies experience this enormous risk that exists in the gap between a linear plan of how we think things are going to be progressing and the exponential rate of actual change. Yet this reality also presents an enormous opportunity, depending on the answer to an alarmingly simple cost–benefit analysis:

The benefit needs to outweigh how much it will cost to change, or the cost of not changing.

So, as you perhaps start to consider the rate of exponential change outside your organization, do you feel that the benefit of changing will outweigh the cost of making that change? Do you feel that the cost of **not** *changing* is a lesser price to pay than the risk that remaining static presents? These should be our primary questions when considering whether to make a change. There should be no emotion attached to it; it is not about whether we want to change or how we feel about change, whether change is hard or whether we tried it before and it didn't work. It's not about whether we've got enough cash to afford it. The decision needs to be based purely on *whether we think the benefit outweighs how much it will cost to change, or the potential cost of not changing.* That's it.

I've found the application of this cost–benefit analysis to be surprisingly rare.

At this point, and as part of that cost–benefit evaluation, I also want you to consider the idea that you may be required to actively disrupt yourself, perhaps even to the point of cannibalizing your existing business in order to mitigate the risk of someone else doing that to you.

At the start of the new millennium the pharmacist-turned-inventor Hon Lik came up with a way of inhaling nicotine without burning the chemicals that are integral parts of the classic cigarette. When he approached the mainstream tobacco companies with this idea, they were unable to see any relevant link to what they did, believing that they were solely in the business of selling cigarettes. These companies looked dismissively at this invention and laughed, in the same way as Kodak looked at Nokia camera phones, and Nokia looked at the Apple iPhone, and BlackBerry looked at all phones . . . They saw it in the same way that Blockbuster video saw Netflix, the music industry saw the internet, the taxi companies saw Uber, and the hotel chains saw Airbnb.

So they did nothing.

Spin forward many years, and it transpires that Imperial Tobacco ended up having to pay out tens of millions of dollars in order to exploit the e-cigarette patents.

The question that I often ask audiences around the world is, "When should the mainstream tobacco companies have taken Hon Lik seriously?" Should that have been when he first approached them, or a year or so later when the idea started to catch on, or the decade down the line when they ended up having to pay out huge amounts to exploit the e-cigarette patents? Of course, the impact of the e-cigarette on the traditional tobacco industry has been a double-digit percentage downturn—and it hurts. Most people's answer to my question is, "At the moment they saw the new invention."

But my argument is different. I would suggest that it should have been a month before they saw it. There is a significant requirement for a company to think about what would potentially disrupt them, and eat into their existing market, *before* they get disrupted. It might feel trite to say that you either need to be the disruptor or be disrupted, but this could make the difference between future success and decline. We will look at the idea of "productive paranoia" later in chapter 9, because it is so important to cultivate the feeling that disruption is always inevitable, and therefore you can be part of creating it if you wish. If we're making strategic bets for the future, then the safest place is to be party to the risk.

I would strongly urge you to ask yourself the following questions:

What would disrupt you?

What is your "e-cigarette"?

What are you fundamentally disregarding as irrelevant today?

What event or factor would mean that the things you are currently doing would no longer be valid in the world?

For Amazon, it would have been the idea of people no longer buying physical books, which is why they created e-ink and disrupted themselves before someone else could disrupt them.

For the tobacco companies, it was the idea of people no longer smoking traditional cigarettes and looking for different ways of getting their nicotine fix, without all of the negative health implications caused by smoking.

It's particularly hard to address those questions when you are experiencing an existing level of success and reward. When things seem to be working, it is very tempting to not do anything. It might feel counterintuitive to suggest that is the exact moment you should be thinking about exactly what could potentially threaten the very existence of your entire operation.

Yet what so often tends to happen is that an organization will intentionally or unintentionally apply what I call "business poisons."

How to build walls

Business poisons are exceptionally popular and extremely dangerous. They make up the component bricks of a wall, attempting to resist or somehow defeat the perpetual and accelerating winds of change.

You may recognize some of the poisons. They sound like this:

"We already know enough so we know about what's going to happen."

"We don't need to know anything more."

"We are fast enough so we will see that something is changing and we will catch up."

"We are good enough, so regardless of what happens we'll be able to eclipse the change anyway."

"We've got enough money in the bank, so we can afford to out-innovate competition."

"We can afford to buy a potentially disruptive company so we will spend our way out of danger."

The pervasiveness of these business poisons, in light of the increasing pace of change, is why once-innovative companies become slow dinosaurs, watching their lunch being eaten by others, because they believe they are innovative enough already. Many organizations also believe that they have plenty of time—but they really don't.

Some firms look around the market and say, *"Nobody else is making proactive changes, therefore nothing is going to happen in our industry."* Or, people look at the region that they operate within and claim, *"It's not going to happen in our country."* These business poisons are similar to other popular, yet unhelpful beliefs such as:

"We tried it before and it didn't work."
"We haven't tried it before so it won't work."
"If we try it then our competitors may see it and get inspired to compete more."
"Our competitors have done it so it won't work for us."
"Our competitors haven't done it so there's no proof it will work for us."
"Our company is different so it won't work for us."
"Our industry is different."
"We have regulations that will stop disruption happening."

I have heard all of these excuses from hundreds of companies over several decades. Then, when they are equipped with counter-evidence and case studies, the following default business poisons also come out: *"That's just not the way we do things here."*

Or, the most popular and most dangerous business poison of all: ***"What's happening isn't relevant to me."***

These business poisons are all variations of how to structure a wall as the winds of change are blowing. Those that build wind-mills actively choose not to let any business poisons take hold, even if some of them begin to creep into the bloodstream of their company. Instead, windmill-makers apply a positive methodology that avoids the poisonous and toxic mindsets that mortally harm wall-builders, and they have remedies in place to ensure that the moment a poison starts to infiltrate their organization, they kill it dead.

An alternative view of "ROI"

One of the main characteristics of wall-builders is a tendency to base future predictions on past realities, especially in terms of return on investment (ROI). When considering ROI, they spend a great deal of time justifying why, in their opinion, the benefit of doing something differently doesn't outweigh the cost of making that change. However, the windmill-makers look at ROI in terms of *risk of inaction*, which requires a fundamentally different mindset. Even though the likely return on investment is still a necessary consideration, having the other definition of ROI constantly in mind guides the speed and persistence with which the windmill is developed.

Next I'll present some tangible examples that clearly illustrate the difference between building a wall and building a windmill, and where an alternative view of ROI—the risk of inaction—could have driven a very different result, had the changes been assessed differently and acted on much faster.

The hotel industry in the last 10 years decided to build a very big wall and then witnessed a fundamental change in the consumption, production, and distribution of its core offering as the advent of the sharing economy and the birth of peer-to-peer room-letting service Airbnb created a competitor that it had not foreseen. It perceived a massive low threat rating across the entire hotel industry and then watched as the inflection point led to mainstream adoption of the changes across their value chain, specifically in the role of the hotel guest who, all of a sudden, could equally be a hotelier themselves.

In my old world, the record industry demonstrated a similar pattern and identical behaviors when faced with the changes in how people accessed and consumed music in an increasingly digital age. And in telecommunications, the mobile networks displayed the same thinking and reactions when the winds of change blew. In their case it was evidenced most strongly in the way that they clung on to their existing model of revenue generated from SMS (text) messages, when confronted with the rise of the free-to-users over-the-top new messaging platforms of players such as WhatsApp, Snapchat, and Instagram.

I find it astonishing that several years after these fundamental changes had taken hold, with their so-often-associated perceived low threat rating, the mobile operators reported that the main challenge in partnering with over-the-top players was the *"inability or difficulty to compete with a fast-growing number of over-the-top market interests."*

It's hard not to feel bemused by this response, given the decade of warning that they had, unless you factor in a generous dose of various business poisons and absolutely no consideration of ROI as the huge, massive, fatal risk of inaction. At this point of inflection into mainstream adoption, a very senior executive of one of the leading mobile network providers even said to me, *"I know the ship is sinking but at least it's my ship."*

Seriously.

I observe a similar pattern across all industry verticals. So many missed opportunities. The tragedy of once-great businesses falling into decline. It is because of this that I believe so strongly in the requirement for us to adopt the "Powered by Change" mentality by thinking more expansively about the way we do business. I'm not advocating total radicalization—let's not fire everyone and burn everything to the ground. But we do need to think more deeply and in different ways about the way we design our companies, and how we do business in this new, ever-changing landscape. Fortunately, over and above my personal experience and conviction that this is the best approach to enable future success, there are other strong arguments for why this should be the case.

Risk and innovation

According to the Insead business school in Paris, 86% of innovation is low-risk and generates 30% of profits, whereas 14% of innovation is radical and generates 70% of company profits.[4] In this context, low-risk innovation is "me too" innovation—for example a phone that's slightly slimmer, with slightly better battery power or a moderately improved camera. Radical innovation meanwhile would involve developing something that removes the requirement for a physical phone altogether, or fundamentally changes the concept itself of what a phone is or how it is used.

We all know what the radical innovation of the iPhone did to companies like Nokia, and how low-risk innovation by Sony and its Walkman range led to the radical innovation of Apple's iPod wiping out Sony's market. This principle goes across all industries, regardless of technological focus.

What "sank" Yahoo? Despite much finger-pointing and "blamestorming," the common consensus is that the leaders stopped taking risks. The same could be said for Nokia, Best Buy, HMV, Blockbuster, and dozens of other examples of companies that got left behind and outmaneuvered by the radical innovations of others that they might not even have considered as competitors until it was too late.

Ultimately, these companies did not build a windmill as the winds of change were blowing. They built very expensive walls. Such walls can take many shapes and come in various sizes. At Microsoft during the leadership of chief executive Steve Ballmer, the company removed 40% of its stock market capitalization in ten years,[5] essentially by assembling an extraordinarily expensive wall constructed with golden bricks. For most of his tenure, he refused to embrace what he deemed the "fad" of cloud-computing technology; he eschewed the idea that consumers would use and like phones without physical keyboards. For the most part, Ballmer also didn't see that there was any need for computer operating systems to be inter-operable, or to create application programming interfaces (APIs) so that other developers could build on top of those platforms. He mostly dismissed those ideas and built a wall around Microsoft when it was the world's largest company, reasoning that it could simply overcome change. What I admire so much about the current CEO (Satya Nadella) is how promotional he has been in the openness of technology. I love the fact that the Outlook app on an iPhone is amazing, and I am entranced by the ability for Dropbox to integrate with Word and PowerPoint. In my opinion, these are the alterations in approach that could enable a share-price growth moving forward, rather than the stark decline of recent years.

It turns out that it just is not possible to achieve perpetual future success by building walls to resist the winds of change. That was not possible for Microsoft, nor for the hotel industry, or for the world of recorded music. It was definitely not a viable option for the video rental market, and it will not work for your businesses, people, and products.

Refresh and review

- Radical **disintermediation** in your business and personal life has only just begun. The force that has already transformed the way you book your flights, travel across town, access holiday accommodation, and order books and furnishings is going to happen in every single industry vertical where supply and demand exists. Stop viewing disintermediation through restrictive "business-to-consumer" and "business-to-business" lenses. It is occurring anywhere that there is a gap between supply and demand that could be shortened or removed, and it is only just beginning to be applied via the Internet of Things and artificial intelligence. Reflect on how your business model could (and likely will) be disrupted by this change. What threat does it bring? How can you instead take advantage of this evolution to make your business not only more resilient but also better at servicing and engaging with customers?

- Through intense **democratization**, your customers can become your competitors as technology is enabling any part of the value chain to play any other part. From "fin-tech" innovations in payment technology to 3D-printing manufacturing, and the expansion and extension of shared-economy retail, democratization means that competitive threat to your business can come from any part of the value chain. Radical democratization is happening in all industry verticals where production, distribution, and consumption exist. Consider how your customers could also provide the services and products that your business offers. How can you respond, as well as begin to think about how your organization can itself move up the chain and challenge its suppliers? Identify the barriers to making this happen and set about dismantling them.

- Far-reaching **disruption**, partly through responses to radical disintermediation and democratization, knows few geographical or societal limits and spreads exponentially. Do not just plan your growth on a linear trajectory, based on simple progression from where your organization currently positions itself. Consider threats from above, below, and alongside you in your markets and supply relationships. How could the dynamics of the industry change to threaten what you offer? How should you be responding? What is it that you do that you can do even better to serve customers more effectively through the things they are increasingly demanding? What technological and other developments are making this possible and what opportunities are there for your business to turn a potential risk into an opportunity?

- Consider the idea that you may be required to actively disrupt yourself before someone else does. Ask yourself these questions:
  – What would disrupt you?
  – What is your "e-cigarette"?
  – What are you fundamentally disregarding as irrelevant today?
  – What would mean that the things you are currently doing would no longer be valid in the world?
  Once you know the answers, consider what you need to do about them. Do the potential threats that you have identified necessitate you hedging your bets about the future by

investing in other technologies or making sure that you have spread your risks in other ways?

- Understand the difference between building walls or windmills in your organization. What do these look and sound like? What business poisons do you hear being given currency by your people? What should you be doing as a business leader about these poisons, and how can you discourage them? How can you reshape the way your people are viewing change, threats, and opportunities in your organization and marketplace, and encourage a more open, responsive, and innovative mindset?

- Take an alternative view of ROI. Actively encourage the costing of "risk of inaction" in your organization alongside the need to consider "return on investment." Remember that the past is not only a poor guide to the future but that this can also be a dangerous way to think, running the risk of misdirecting resources, missing opportunities, and falling behind new and developing competitors. Develop a matrix to contextualize what is happening in your world or marketplace, and how those changes could transform your industry. Work out the risks of failing to adapt to this new development or trend. Ensure that "risk of inaction" is given enough weight and consideration, together with your standard ROI measurement and models.

CHAPTER FOUR

Structuring Our Responses

The issue of how to survive and thrive as an organization in a time of perpetual change is the most important problem that any company faces, and how firms act on it is the most important decision they make. Yet the question as to *how* most businesses do counter this threat to their very existence can be summed up in two words. They don't.

Most companies choose to simply live for the next quarter or financial year. The chief executive is probably not going to be around for more than five years, so he or she inevitably sees his or her responsibility ending there. That's also how CEO bonuses and so-called "long-term incentive plans" are structured, so it follows that corporate action plans are geared to three-year turnarounds and five-year growth plans. A CEO who has delivered consistent growth for five years is hailed as a hero in the City. Nobody asks how he or she intends to safeguard the company's future in the face of exponential change. I encounter this problem regularly in my consultancy work. When I tell chief executives that nine out of ten of the companies who choose inaction in the face of perpetual change will go out of business over a 30- to 40-year period, their response is inevitably that it will not be their problem. The human ego is programmed to act in its own self-interest over its own limited lifetime. Even family companies often do not think long-term enough, with differences in attitude over the length of outlook a major cause of internecine warfare. Sadly, the exemplary chief executives like Unilever's Paul Polman who scrap quarterly reporting because they want to run their companies with a longer-term mindset are all too rare.

Since becoming Unilever chief executive in 2009, Dutchman Paul Polman has made a commitment to position the consumer-goods company around the generation of long-term sustainability, rather than pure shareholder value.

One of his early actions was to abandon Unilever's quarterly reporting of its financial results on the basis that it was too short-termist. He moved the employee share scheme's goalposts from three to five years for the same reason.

For Polman, the driving force is alignment with customers, with genuine shareholder returns produced when the company understands its consumers intimately and reflects their concerns by operating responsible, purpose-driven brands.

He has put purpose at the heart of Unilever, making public statements on human rights, violence and discrimination against women, sustainable development, and infrastructure and climate change. Polman claims that the Unilever brands that meet the highest standards for social and environmental impact are growing 40% faster than the group's other products.

This philosophy came under pressure in early 2017 with Unilever coming under attack from some shareholders who were anxious for more growth.

However, a surprise bid approach from American rival Kraft Heinz ironically played into Polman's hands, with the US company easily caricatured as displaying the opposite kind of capitalism to Unilever's. The bid idea was dropped and Polman's plan has been given more time to reap dividends.

The actions of those who do reply to the threat fall into two camps: those who choose to *react* to the reality of perpetual change and those who elect to *respond* to it. These are very different actions. A reaction is what we do immediately after experiencing something; it's a re-enactment of something that we have programmed ourselves to do. A response is about equipping ourselves with the mindsets to constantly be able to adapt to changes that we cannot possibly completely foresee.

Success in a world of perpetual change is response-dependent, whether the choice is between being a victim or being a survivor, between being bullied or taking action about it, or between looking at the internet as a threat or an opportunity, Humans can adapt once they understand the problem and decide to act, but when they do, the default option is often one of reaction—or what so often seems to result in building a wall.

I have been guilty of this too, of course. For instance, in one of the early companies I launched, I was faced with a choice of automating a task that historically had been done by several members of staff. My past experience had been that automation was not very efficient, as it had historically created more issues than it solved. My reaction was, therefore, "Automation won't work; let's hire more staff to carry out the task."

I wasn't taking into account the fact that modern technology had increased in capability and affordability—so the context of the earlier decisions was now fundamentally different, even irrelevant, to this current problem I was facing. My chosen response should have been, "Let's investigate whether today's automation could do that job more efficiently, regardless of my historic experiences." As it turned out, my reaction of completely ignoring a potential alternative outcome, and avoiding automation, was a bad choice, as my competitors stole advantage by using modern automation for things I was using many staff to do at a much slower pace and for a lot more money.

To quote Viktor Frankl once again, "Between stimulus and response there is a space. In that space is our power to choose our response. In our response lies our growth and our freedom." *It is our choice of response that makes all the difference.*

I'm going to give you a high-level view of some of the changes that are happening in the modern landscape, at the current time of writing in 2017. As I do so, please be aware of and consider your reaction as you read. Remember that if we are ultimately in the game of building windmills, then we need to be actively responding to change rather than just reacting to it.

To start us off, let's look at the changes in connectivity. At the current time of writing, we're living in a world where four billion people are connected to smart devices. In a few years' time, it will be up to 75% of the world's population. What that actually means in terms of connectivity is that we're no longer hierarchically down the value chain from companies. We are now more connected than companies themselves. In fact, every single person who has a smart device, or connected device, is linked to an average of 120 people who form their first-tier "reach."

The second-tier reach of these connected people is 120 times the 120 people that those contacts are connected to, which is 14,400. The third-tier reach is 14,400 times each of their 120 connections, which is 1.728 million people. This means that every single digitally connected person has a third-tier media reach that rivals that of any organization!

This isn't just related to marketing capabilities but to every part of the value chain. The population is not only super-powered; it is also super-connected. It is worth noting that the world's digitally enabled population isn't really up to only the seven billion or so individuals alive today, because people have multiple online personas. So someone will have one persona on one channel, another on a different channel, and others elsewhere. Add this to the average connections we can reach and we can see the huge changes in our contexts of connectivity.

Product development challenges

Let's take a moment to examine the changes happening in new product development. One illustration is that of Procter & Gamble with its "Connect + Develop" initiative,[6] which has created a crowdsourced innovation platform that up to 40% of its new products go through, and with up to a million people collaborating at any one time.

Unilever has its own platform, called "Foundry,"[7] and many other companies are now also duplicating this approach, even though this general concept has been around for almost 10 years. There has been a lot of business poison involved in those companies looking at it and saying, "We don't work like that." However, market-leading companies have achieved measurable, demonstrable success from crowdsourcing, and that then makes an argument strong enough to eventually beat away such arguments.

In the area of investment, we are experiencing a situation where the public is increasingly becoming a superpower in the financing landscape. One example involves an American comedy series called *Mystery Science Theatre 3000*. Some $2 million was needed to bring back the series, yet 48,270 backers pledged $5,764,229 to help bring this project to life.[8] You may think that's just an anomaly, but at the time there were 53,000 other film and TV projects that were also raising funding on Kickstarter.

In general finance, we're in an interesting situation where there are two billion people who have mobile phones but no bank accounts. This results in an enormous market opportunity in micro-payments, micro-credits, micro-savings, and micro-insurance. Yet most of the time, these aren't even seen as being interesting or viable by people who are either in the finance industry or the mobile-phone industry.

Ironically, the majority of mobile-phone companies have always resisted being banks, despite the fact that they are blatantly suited to be them. I suspect that by the time they do work out they need to be banks, the banking industry will be disrupted by something called blockchain and it will be too late for many of them.

In the simplest terms, a blockchain is a distributed database that maintains a continuously growing list of records called blocks secured from tampering and revision. Each block contains a timestamp and a link to a previous block. Known by many as the technology underpinning the Bitcoin digital currency, blockchain has acquired a new identity in more mainstream enterprise. At a time when companies face new challenges in data management and security, it's emerging as a way to let companies make and verify transactions on a network instantaneously without a central authority.

Some companies see an opportunity to use blockchain to track the movement of assets throughout their supply chains or electronically initiate and enforce contracts. In actual fact, I find it hard to imagine many cases where this technology couldn't be applied. Whether it's corporate bonds, securities issuance, settlement risk, financial inclusion, operational risk, crowdfunding, or even syndicated loans, I have a hunch that a lot of the world as we currently know it will be fundamentally redesigned by this free-of-charge, open-source software called the blockchain.

These are major changes, and remember, we can either react or we can respond.

As an exercise, consider your views on the following three areas of genuine transformative change. Will you react to these examples, or will you respond—and how will you do so?

1) THE DEMOCRATIZATION OF PRODUCTION

Imagine that you are in production, where companies like Electroloom and Foodini have started the processes of democratizing the manufacturing process. With Electroloom you could create any piece of clothing you like using your Electroloom machine. You designed a mold, put the ingredients into the machine, pressed Print, and your garment got made. That specific company has now shut down,[9] but is a perfect example of an early player in the space of consumer technology, enabling anyone to be a fashion-garment manufacturer.

Foodini uses a similar process but with food, enabling you to print out items of food, from burgers to pasta.[10]

These changes in manufacturing process and capability are impacting other industries as well—for example in Dubai, where there's an entire building that's made by 3D printers;[11] the 21,000 buildings in Egypt that have been commissioned to be built using 3D-printing technology;[12] and an entire housing estate of luxury mansions in China that have been printed.[13] This is a major wind of change, but unsurprisingly most manufacturers and building firms are still choosing to stick to their well-built walls—metaphorically and literally. Do you react to this? Or do you respond? How are the two actions different?

2) THE END OF OWNERSHIP

In another part of the value chain we can see that the very concept of ownership has fundamentally changed. My daughter thinks that my vinyl records are where I "store my downloads." Services like Spotify mean that people don't actually need to own any music. Zipcar, and its many competitors, has meant that people don't need to own or even rent cars in the traditional way.

Interestingly, the whole idea of ownership is already in decline. Airbnb, the largest accommodation provider, owns no real estate. Facebook, the largest content provider, owns no content. Uber, the largest vehicle pool, owns no vehicles, and Alibaba, the largest retailer, owns no inventory. It seems that even in business, the concept of ownership has changed.

On the consumer side, most entertainment is consumed upon platforms that aren't necessarily owned by the consumer, and many services used, whether they are utilities or software licenses, aren't owned but rented. The entire idea of ownership has already changed. What hasn't, yet, is the general understanding of self-capitalism in a democratized value chain—in other words, the awareness within the general public that capitalist growth is at their individual disposal, regardless of traditional corporations. I predict that once that level of understanding has risen, we will witness more industrial growth within our society than in standard business. In my opinion that's the major paradigm shift up next in this context. Do you react to this change? Or do you respond to it? How do those two actions differ?

3) REALITY IS BECOMING VIRTUAL

The changes we are witnessing in the domain of relationships mean that there are hotels now where you can actually bring along your virtual girlfriend or virtual boyfriend.[14] You can also go and watch a live concert with a rapper who is alive, dancing next to and interacting with a hologram of a rapper who is dead.[15] You can actually buy tickets for that. At one of these holographic concerts, the hologram itself was arrested—in this case for speaking out against the US.

If we take all of that just one step further, these evolutions feel like nothing in comparison to what's happening with touchable, haptic holographics that allow you to actually feel and interact with holograms.[16] How might you react to this development? And how might you respond instead? What is the difference?

The future is here now

Nothing that I've written about here is futuristic; all of it exists at the time of writing in 2017, even if those things are not yet widely distributed within the mainstream markets. To understand what's going on around us does however require a curious mind, and a commitment to continually improve your knowledge about the changes and evolutions taking place across industry and technology.

To give a little more context to some of these changes, bear in mind that up until 1994, businesses were only required to view customers as being those people who walked into your shop or into your farm, who sent you a letter, or called you on the phone. The advent of the World Wide Web meant that the context in which we do business fundamentally changed from being only local, to being global and local (or "glocal," which is a term I loathe!)—but essentially our customer base and supplier relationships stopped being linked just to where we were physically in proximity, or the phone calls we made. As customers, we were now able to look at the stock options a supplier listed on a website, or we could buy a piece of sheet music from our local retailer who was actually reselling that piece of sheet music from an international supplier. Indeed, I was one of the first people in the world to ever do that! That contextual change from however far back you go until 1994 was a major shift when we look at everything that happened after that time.

The next technological shift is in the whole area of under-the-skin technology. So, we had human-to-human, then we had human and machine, and now we're going to have machine in human. While a lot of commentators will be scared of machines owning humans and that whole dystopian view, I suspect that we are already in the world of self-tracking and conversational links.

To give you a really basic example, at the moment, in 2017, you can track your heart rate, your blood pressure, your body's salt content, and your metabolism in certain ways. The database that's recording that information is the company that sold you the machinery. But by around 2020, moving forward, I suspect that your own personal information and preferences will be directly linked to the product that you buy. So you will be able to go onto a web store, or to the digital retailer of your choice, and when you arrive there the "concierge" is actually the device that has been recording your internal metabolic rate. In turn, the products that you choose will be filtered down based on what is already known to suit you. This is due to the fact that the filtering process already exists underneath your skin. Therefore, with an elevated mindset, you can now ask how you could add real additional value when you have access to that level of the most personal information. Increasingly, we are going to find ourselves inside a business context of having access to the most personal, DNA-based information that we can potentially choose to apply when creating any future products and services.

Did you know, for example, that a Scandinavian bio-hacking company has developed a sensor chip that is put underneath a human arm to enable scientists to read what's happening inside a person and relate it to the outside world?[17] Elsewhere, there is innovation around "smart dust"—new cameras that are the size of a grain of salt. They can be swallowed, take pictures of human organs, and view the way that the body operates. When you are aware of these evolutions, you can then consider how you can apply your knowledge of these inventions to generate additional value within your industry and marketplace.

What would it mean for your company if you could download a brand-new language in real time, or enable five billion people to become coders of your software in a day? Scientists already know how to upload knowledge to people's brains through neuro-stimulation.[18] This is the definition of value-adding disruption.

Other things that already exist are the DNA nanobots that can go under your skin, into your body, and fix you up.[19] Smart medicine, sometimes also called digital smart medicine, was FDA-approved in 2012 and is produced by a company called Proteus Digital Health.[20]

This smart medicine currently comes in the form of pills you can consume; the pills will then send their findings to any connected machine and assess your general health patterns. They will give you an evaluation of the effectiveness of your medication, and they are even starting to be used as a supporting diagnostic tool. 3D-printed pills are another example, enabling you to print out your own drugs.

I imagine that you will already be well aware that today we're in a situation where artificial intelligence is raising questions such as, "How far away are robot overlords that want to take over the human race?" There is an ever-increasing number of start-ups that are aiming to transfer our consciousness into artificial bodies, so that we can have the potential to live forever.[21] At the same time, scientists are gleefully searching for ways that AI can evolve so that they possess their own, independent, decision-making skills.

We are increasingly seeing changes in ethics where hackers are launching balloons to spy on drones and getting arrested.[22] Dads are getting arrested for shooting down drones hovering over their daughters and taking pictures.[23] These examples only begin to scratch the surface of the issues that we are facing more and more in our new-look society.

Some people have no ethical problem with programming insects to do what they want, at the same time as others are programming robots to take over humans. The developing field of cryonics[24] meanwhile allows individuals to be frozen just before death. In theory, this gives them the chance of living forever if they are ever able to be awakened when things have progressed far enough to provide solutions, cures, and remedies.

Meanwhile, Google and Arthur D. Levinson launched a project called "Calico" in 2013 with the highly ambitious goal of "curing death."[25] Scientists have already claimed that they can extend life "way beyond the age of 120 years."[26] The Indian billionaire entrepreneur and philanthropist Tej Kohli, who is busy with his goal to eradicate the corneal blindness that currently afflicts 46 million people in the world by 2035, confidently believes that his 16-year-old son will live to the age of at least 125, if not 150.[27]

When we take a moment to observe some of the changes happening in employment, it's not hard to find commentary on and examples of the huge shifts that are taking place. Oxford University believes that 47% of US jobs are under threat.[28] The Bank of England foresees that the jobs most at risk are those that are in sales and customer service, unskilled trades, care, leisure, service, and some skilled trades as well.[29] Most technology experts and social commentators believe that artificial intelligence (AI) will have a transformative impact across industry, business, and society.

If this is indeed inevitable, our focus then changes to how we can prepare for the changes that these evolutions will bring. "Make no mistake," warns Shelly Palmer, chief executive of technology consultancy The Palmer Group. "At some level, every job can and will be done by machine. It's not a question of if; it's just a question of when.

"If you're wondering where your job sits on the list of 'Run for your life, the robots are coming,' you have a simple, singular mission," Palmer adds. "Learn how your job is going to be automated. Learn everything about what your job will become and become the very best machine partner you can. Everyone will tell you that none of this is happening any time soon. They are flat wrong."[30]

The roles and positions that are considered to be less under threat have been calculated as being managers, directors, and senior officials. However, this ignores the fact that there are examples where algorithms have been appointed as board directors since 2014.[31]

Foxconn, which makes Apple products, fired 60,000 people and replaced them with robots.[32]

Peter, an AI-based business lawyer,[33] claims to be used by a member of Facebook's staff, while Ross, another AI lawyer created by IBM, also has clients.[34] You can include Ross or Peter in your emails and they will produce contracts in a fraction of a second, utilizing the entire knowledge of every single law that's ever been passed on record. Looking at this, it would appear that there are major likely disruptions to the future of the legal profession.

When we look at the bigger picture, just these few changes that I have highlighted here can easily be applied to pretty much any industry area of your choosing, and they are therefore likely to impact the future of all doctors, all nurses, all car builders, all mail carriers, all post office workers, all retailers, all restaurant workers, all delivery companies, all tourism providers . . . All of us.

Consider the technological possibilities of riding roughshod over personal human rights and our private spaces that are offered up by the latest public cameras and recording devices that can remotely track pretty much everything that everybody does. This throws up enormous social and libertarian questions about regulation, policing, and who guards the guards. An exploitative mindset with regard to the opportunities that these types of developments present could have catastrophic consequences. But if we truly seek to comprehend how any of these things **could enable us to add even more value**, that minimizes those risks by making us naturally unexploitative. This is fundamentally important for societal stability and security.

Do you see the difference between the way you could have reacted defensively, incredulously, or dismissively to the changes I have just described, or with a measured, progressive response that sees all change as opportunity and pauses only to figure out how to effect the best competitive reply? It is a difference that is going to grow even more important in the years ahead because our response times are going to have to shorten dramatically.

In my view, today is the slowest pace of change we'll ever experience. The only option for a productive and successful future is to choose to build a windmill when the winds of change are blowing.

In part 2, I will explain how businesses can design, structure, and build their own windmills to utilize, benefit from, and be actively powered by these changes. Like many windmills, those that are going to drive our future success have four equal blades, but building them will involve embedding in each blade three vital sections that will equip them with the strength, flexibility, and durability to withstand and prosper from the fiercest winds that can ever attempt to blow them away.

Refresh and review

Structuring our responses involves using the space between a stimulus, such as a change or an event, and action on that stimulus to reflect, evaluate, and make a reasoned choice. Take time after identifying the trends that are going to blow your world apart to plan how your organization will be able to survive and thrive in those circumstances. And start by considering the winds that are already blowing.

Think deeply about how your business will cope with:

- the explosion in personal and corporate **connectivity**;

- the decline of **ownership** and rise of social-rental models;

- the relentless march of **artificial intelligence**;

- the increasing use of **3D printing**;

- advances in **healthcare**, increased longevity, and a resulting older demographic profile;

- the changing nature and value of **jobs** and humans in the workforce.

These are just a few examples of transformative winds of change that are already blowing. How you structure your organization's response will determine how it is able to survive and prosper, using these forces for benefit, rather than being destroyed by them. But in your preparations, are you building walls to resist them or windmills that are actively powered by them?

Process

- Frameworks
- Filtration
- Co-ordination

Purpose

- Elevation
- Specification
- Integration

Product

- Candles versus Mirrors
- Transposition
- Mess-finding

People

- Skill and Will
- Productive Paranoia
- The Paradox of Exploitation versus Exploration

PART 2

How to Build Windmills

How to Build Windmills

TAs I mentioned right at the start, I call the strategic thinking that I have developed and that underpins this book the "Windmill Theory." Windmills have blades that rotate when they are hit by winds. Change doesn't destroy them or knock them over; it enables them to move and to produce benefits from that movement. In our windmill, four equal blades work in a cohesive, integrated way in order to harness the winds of change and use them to our advantage, producing beneficial results as we are powered by the winds of perpetual change.

Those four main component parts, the four "blades" of our windmill, are these:

Blade 1: The first blade is **purpose**: what we do, how we do it, and why it matters.

Blade 2: The second blade is about having the optimal **people** inside the organization.

Blade 3: The third blade is the **product** or service we are offering.

Blade 4: The fourth blade is **process**: enabling the other three blades to function.

These are the four blades of the windmill design that enables organizations to survive and thrive in a world of perpetual change. If you do not have these four blades functioning well in your company, I do not think that you will see out another decade as a business. This is not an exaggeration. Structuring your ability to respond to change in this way is the only effective approach of trying to safeguard your future.

There are many nuances of businesses that can be adjusted to help cope with change. My observation, however, is that the companies that do best in the face of change always have a combination of an absolutely clear purpose and a collection of the best people, who are all aligned with that purpose. They also always have a product or service that fixes a mess or adds so much value in the marketplace that people would be majorly disadvantaged to be without it. In addition, they always have a range of processes that allow the entire organization to run in a purposeful, productive, and efficient way. Of course, it helps if a company faces into the oncoming winds of change with a bankload full of cash. This can make organizations braver and enable more risk-taking. Yet it is absolutely not an essential requirement. There are plentiful examples of firms that managed to build effective windmills to be powered by change without much money set aside. There are even more instances of companies that were reckless with the cash they had and the borrowings they could muster, and totally failed to spend it on pursuing the right opportunities in ways that allowed these four blades to rotate harmoniously and effectively.

All of these four blades have to be inter-operable or the windmill won't function. They need to work in synchrony with one another, and removing just one blade will cause an organization to experience a negative outcome. If the Purpose blade is removed, we end up with a company full of confusion because no one understands why things are being done. If you remove the People blade, it results in a vast amount of frustration and resistance because the leaders and employees inside the firm are suboptimal. If you remove the Product blade, you risk bankruptcy due to not having something viable to sell and make any profit from. And if you unilaterally remove the Process blade, nothing functions as well as it could, and ideas and innovation wither away.

Everything in business needs to have the four blades working in harmony. Turning together, they drive an empowered organization that uses the winds of change as a powering mechanism for optimal success. As this may seem obvious, one could be tempted to wonder why these blades aren't constantly kept optimized inside a company, so that as change happens it becomes the very thing that fuels success.

I have spent years wondering why that is the case, and have come to understand the answer in this way. When a car has an undiagnosed problem resulting in underperformance and goes into a garage to get serviced, the mechanic will normally put the car on a ramp, in order to undertake a diagnostic session. An initial assessment is carried out. The first way of assessing a problem is to look at why the car doesn't work. The mechanics tend to start with the macro picture first and then go into the micro, the smaller problems.

In business, we can take the same approach when we are trying to understand the reason for the failure to adopt a "powered-by-change" practice. We need to first start with the wider view, or macro perspective, and then drill down into the myriad smaller nuances.

Diagnosing the problem

From a wider perspective, it is almost always a mindset, or viewpoint problem. It comes down to the mindset around our purpose, the way that our thinking about that purpose can percolate through our people, and how their mindsets can create the products and the services we offer, and in turn the application of the processes that enable our businesses to run.

So, if we look at a business from the viewpoint of a leader who is trying to change its culture but does not understand why it is the way that it is, looking at the problem in terms of micro issues will focus on facets such as a lack of daylight in an office, the rudeness of staff, the lack of free coffee, or the fact that a company's products have boring names.

Behind the scenes, however, my experience is that the bigger picture always has to do with the way we think about the business we're in, and the people we work with, and the things that we offer, and the way in which we do it. These are the four blades of purpose, people, product, and process, but they don't get built automatically; they need the constituent parts that we are going to explain in the second half of this book. Without the right mindset and approach, building and maintaining the necessary blades becomes very hard to do in practice, regardless of how obvious the necessity to do so appears in theory. This is why organizations find it so difficult to shape and develop themselves in ways that allow change to be embraced as a constant and also as a perpetual opportunity—an ever-present chance to improve businesses, the people in them, the things they make, and the way that they do so. It is not about improvement for improvement's sake. It is betterment that is necessary and vital if change is not to destroy our organizations.

The make-up of the blades

As for how each blade is constructed, they are all built with three parts. These sections are in logical order and enable the winds of change to flow through and power the windmill as a whole. Even if you feel that one or more of these sections is covered adequately in your business, the real challenge is to look at the entirety of the 12 sections and judge whether or not all of them are covered *equally well*. Only then can we say that an organization is optimally designed and rigorously structured in the face of perpetual change.

There is also a logic to the order in which the blades need to be built and assembled. If companies set out in business without a clearly defined notion of what they are trying to achieve, it is astronomically difficult to attract the best employees. It is true that getting the right people could enable a better purpose to be found, but it is unlikely that such people will turn up if they do not know why they should care. The "people-cart" cannot move unless there is a "purpose-horse" in front of it, a road that it is on, and a direction in which to travel. That's what I mean by the purpose of a business, and that's the first blade that companies need to build if they want to be adaptive and responsive to perpetual change.

Ordering of the blades

In logical order: a company requires good leaders to establish their purpose in order to attract the best talent to bring their business to life. That "bringing to life" is achieved through the creation and delivery of optimum products (or services) driven by the purpose-fuelled people who are in place, and with the necessary processes that enable all of these to continually happen in the most efficient way. All of this ultimately means that the organization will be more far more future-proof than it otherwise would be.

In this part of the book, we will look in detail at each of the sections of the four blades and how they are conceived, designed, constructed, and combined to work together.

Blade One
PURPOSE

Purpose is the first blade that we work to construct, because it forms the foundation and meaning for all the others. To build it involves paying attention to its constituent sections of *elevation*, *specification*, and *integration*. But first I want to define what we mean by purpose, and the part it plays when it comes to building agility and adaptability in order to survive and thrive in this world of perpetual change.

It is worth really getting to the heart of this, because I want to somewhat challenge the way that purpose is traditionally perceived. Getting to grips with the purpose of a business is commonly understood to mean looking at **why** it should exist, and then building engagement and loyalty on the back of that mission along with the values that underpin it. This can be a fruitful exercise, and it has also become linked to the corporate sustainability agenda, which is no bad thing. As Virgin Group founder Sir Richard Branson says, "If you are building a business without purpose, not only are you missing the point, but you are most likely missing out on the journey, the excitement and the profit too."[35]

Unilever's Paul Polman, the flag-bearer of the purpose movement or zeitgeist, puts it slightly differently but still sees purpose in business as being fundamentally about the "why." "The best businesses understand their consumer intimately," he says. "They are real people with complex lives and concerns. That's why the market for responsible, purpose-driven brands is growing so rapidly. There's a massive return for companies on these social investments. We need to step up and deliver . . . through genuinely purpose-driven brands that answer a real need."[36]

I have no argument with either of these views. There is some clear evidence that the 2008 financial crisis has left a residue of doubt about the rationale and functioning of the capitalist system, and a need for a stated purpose that entails more than simple profits and shareholder value. However, the requirement for this is not new. In ancient civilizations, such questions were asked too. Indeed, in ancient Greece, individuals' tombstones recorded not the dates of the deceased's birth and death but the thing that defined their "*telos*," or the essential purpose of their very being. Teleology was a major subject, and in those days the searchers of reason were regarded as leaders and superheroes. So we can see that the questioning of purpose goes back a very long way. Over time, it has been more and more commoditized, and maybe it does indeed take crises and crashes to give it new vigor and life. One just hopes that the latest resurgence of interest can be sustained, as it is such a critically important topic.

However, the approach to purpose that I want to talk about here is linked more closely to the "what" than to the "why" of a business. Ethical approaches to businesses are commendable and worthy, and it is hard to argue with the conviction that those firms that do not operate in line with consumers' moral compasses greatly diminish their chances of survival. However, being ethical or clear about your "why" does not automatically guarantee continued success in a perpetually changing world, which is what this book is concerned with.

When we look ahead to the changes that will transform the planet in the next 10 or 20 years, if we truly want to be able to adapt, then a company's purpose needs to be framed around *"what"* it is for as much as it does about *"why"* it is doing it. One might think that some of the world's biggest companies would know exactly what it is they do, if not precisely why they do it. Yet a first glance at this can miss what is actually at the heart of a company's reason for existence.

CHAPTER FIVE

Elevation

Elevation is the ability to go deep into the heart of what a company's purpose is truly about, in order to then raise our sights and identify the opportunities for growth. This clarity can make an organization agile enough to take advantage of the opportunities that get blown in by the winds of change. Elevation is effectively the non-myopic version of what it is that you do. It is the wider or higher perspective of the business that you're in. It can be understood as soon you see that firefighters, for example, aren't actually in the business of putting out fires; they're in the business of saving lives. It is really helpful to think of an elevated purpose as the outcome—the overall outcome benefit—of what it is that we do.

Elevation is the way of describing our purpose from a wider perspective that isn't limited to one particular activity. The problem nowadays is that we're addicted to activities, and we describe things almost exclusively in terms of tasks. The challenge that creates is that when we simply describe things purely as tasks, we limit our potential for innovation by imposing the boundaries of that very specific activity.

For instance, if we believe that we are in the business of selling loft ladders, then we can only sell loft ladders. That's what we do. If we're in the business of mortgages, then we can only ever create better mortgages. If we can elevate, however, then we can push out and widen those boundaries, and we can access far more limitless opportunities.

Failure to elevate is one of the biggest reasons for companies failing to survive the winds of perpetual change, or being reduced by these to mere shadows of their former selves. In the music industry, the CD-manufacturing companies are one of the most obvious examples of this. They believed they were in the business of CDs, focusing only on making better and better CDs. If they had realized that they were really in the business of entertainment, then they would not have run this permanent risk of disruption, and actually what they would have done is created MP3 players, and digital downloads, and iTunes—whereas in fact what they did was create better and better CDs. So yes, by all means, carry out those tasks, fish where there are fish, make more CDs—but be aware of the fact that across every single industry vertical known to man, from the original cognitive revolution of 70,000 years ago, to the agricultural revolution of 12,000 years ago, to the start of the first industrial revolution 1,000 years ago, right up until now, all we can see are perpetual cycles of disruption. We therefore either need to become a disruptor ourselves, or if we opt out of that, then we are effectively choosing to be disrupted. Then it becomes simply a matter of when that moment will come, and that looks like a pretty high-risk strategy.

Let's take Harley-Davidson as another example of an elevated purpose. What is it for? What is the reason for its existence? The company sells iconic American motorbikes, right? As the best-known of the two major American motorbike companies to survive the Great Depression of the 1930s, it has grown into an international behemoth, with a devoted army of followers and even a company-sponsored, brand-focused Harley-Davidson museum.

Yet when we apply elevation to understand the true purpose of what it is that Harley-Davidson does, we can see that the company is not actually in the business of selling motorbikes. It is in the business of something much, much greater, which means that it can diversify in multiple ways with multiple million-dollar opportunities. Merchandise, drive-through cafés, restaurants, hotels, skateboards, leather jackets, whiskey ... Harley-Davidson now does all these things, none of which jar at all with its consumer base. Why? Because the company has *elevated* its business thinking and operations to discover its *"main thing"*—its true purpose of existence. Harley-Davidson does not think that it is primarily in the business of selling motorbikes. Its main thing, seen from an elevated position, is *enabling the experience of freedom.* The reason it can provide that full range of services and products that it now does is because it has elevated its thinking, and has clarity of what it is absolutely in the business of: enabling the experience of freedom.

Knowing what your main thing is enables you to see numerous opportunities from a higher, elevated perspective.

If we take a moment to consider the "second coming" of Apple that was one of the corporate success stories of the first decade of this century, we can see that its co-founder Steve Jobs had a very clear purpose for the company, which was all about its position at the intersection of industrial design and the creative arts. His background in calligraphy gave him an understanding of how to couple beauty and structured elegance—and the result is his legacy to the company today. It enabled Apple to move from Macintosh desktops to iPod music players and mobile phones, making the leap from computing to telecoms effortlessly because its elevated purpose can be defined as being fundamentally about designing beautiful products that people love. I, for one, am glad that the company's progress and development was not restricted by a non-elevated view that it was just in the business of selling computers.

Similarly, Wonderbra is able to be associated with huge initiatives all over the world that are not directly linked to selling underwear because this company has also elevated its purpose. Wonderbra does not see itself as simply being in the business of selling lingerie. Its main thing is helping to *instill self-confidence.* Wonderbra can choose to get involved with any service, product, or idea that helps to bring about a greater sense of self-confidence, without any brand confusion whatsoever.

In sportswear, Nike chief executive Mark Parker is clear that the company's overriding purpose[37] is to "bring inspiration and innovation to every athlete in the world." If you read that and feel that the definition of the target audience sounds narrow, add to this official company purpose the qualification of "athlete" that was made by the company's co-founder Bill Bowerman: "If you have a body, you are an athlete," was Bowerman's observation.[38] It could hardly be more inclusive. As for any new inventions or initiatives that they choose to launch, because they are clear about being in the game of bringing inspiration and innovation to every athlete in the world, as long as there is a fit within that elevated purpose then they are likely to succeed.

But let's not avoid the knotty issues of all the companies that do have a clearly defined purpose, but still appear vulnerable to some of the macroeconomic changes that we identified back in chapter 3. Uber, for example, was founded with the primary purpose of exploiting the disintermediation that was obvious in the taxi and personal transportation market, by linking surplus to demand in an accessible way. However, the company has been distracted of late by the abrasive style of its founder Travis Kalanick, who resigned as chief executive in June 2017, remaining on the board. Some detractors argue that the company has lost sight of its purpose and is not powered by the winds of change. It will certainly be interesting to see if Uber, under new leadership, is able to re-state its purpose and resonate once again with its people and the governments of the territories where it operates. For a while, at least, the company seems to be forgetting its key stakeholders. In a similar way, coupons innovator Groupon faltered after rapid growth in its early years because it neglected the retailers it was formed to serve.

An elevated purpose does not have to be ethical. But if the perceived or even stated purpose of an organization is simply to make as much money as possible, all the three other blades of the windmill would be disadvantaged and less successful. The company will attract people who are purely there to make money, probably for themselves. It will then make products that add little societal value other than making a bucketload of profit. And the corporate process of such a firm will be solely about extracting as much cash from society as possible for the benefit of the company. How will such a business be resilient to trends such as the focus of Millennials on sustainability, community, and social footprints? What will be the resulting effects on the recruitment, retention, and engagement of the best talent? And how will such a company go about convincing customers that they should buy more of its products purely to enrich the board and the shareholders? These are rhetorical questions before the answers are clear. Such a company is highly susceptible to being swept away or left behind by the winds of change.

There are some sectors, such as investment banking, where simple profit has been seen in the past as a perfectly respectable pursuit, though that came under serious threat in the aftermath of the 2008 financial crisis. If one were asked to define the elevated purpose of Goldman Sachs, moreover, it would not be credible to express what the company is in any other way than to state that it is there to provide regular and growing returns to financial shareholders. Does that make the company any less sustainable? Not necessarily. But would Goldman be more future-proofed if it could distribute the message that it has found a better way of funding public infrastructure, or perhaps has developed a solution to the many problems presented by Bitcoin? Would those examples of a more elevated purpose resonate with a wider range of stakeholders across more levels of society over a longer term? I would suggest that this is exactly what would happen. Goldman has also demonstrated that it understands this, by running programs that encourage staff to take part in community volunteering projects on company time. Even when the over-riding purpose is to make profits, there is room to focus on the greater good.

To have the best possible chance of surviving into the future, a business is not required to be morally righteous, but a purpose does need to benefit more than simply its owner. Imagine an Uber whose stated purpose was to enable people to monetize their surplus resource. If that were the case, wouldn't the company also see the opportunity of extending its business model, for example to solve the mess of food companies throwing away perfectly good produce at the end of each day, and then linking that resource to the problems of homelessness and poverty?

But there are lessons here for more than simply a perceived bad boy of the sharing economy. Is Apple at risk of having its supply-chain issues with contractors seep so far into the public consciousness that customers no longer view its products as being made with an ethos that cross-sections industrial beauty with artistic design? What if the disseminated purpose is seen instead as merely a desire to constantly upgrade their highly priced products, and therein swell the company's already gigantic cash reserves? How would that affect Apple's legions of die-hard fans, and what would the likely results be to the company's balance sheet?

It is easy for cynics to scoff at stated purposes and to see them simply as public-relations statements that legitimize otherwise questionable corporate behavior pursued for a pure capitalistic motivation such as profit. However, my experience is that there is usually genuine belief in an elevated company purpose within the senior leadership. Anyone who has worked with Jesper Brodin at IKEA will report that he holds a zealous conviction in the company's purpose of making a better life at home for many people. It is a true belief that drives the company's behaviors and decisions, rather than a strapline or nice piece of marketing spiel.

True elevation of purpose is what makes businesses really sustainable into the future—in the sense that they are able to carry on being in existence for longer, and survive and thrive more than they otherwise would. To state it once again, this is all about having the clarity of what their main thing is, and what they are really, truly in the business of doing when viewed from an elevated position.

Here's another example of that in action for you. The entrepreneur Elon Musk is commonly known for trying to land people on Mars, put drivers in electric cars through his Tesla company, and build cities that are powered by the sun. But Musk is on a much bigger mission. He has elevated. The purpose of what he is all about is completely clear. If we wanted to compete with his companies by trying to make better electric cars, trying to build a better rocket ship, or installing solar energy sources into cities, we'd find the competitive landscape confusing, as he's not in the business of those three things. His main thing is *preserving humanity*. He's elevated up to a position where the opportunities are endless. Tesla has realized what its elevated purpose is and dropped the word "Motors" from its name because that's not what it's just about anymore. If you want to compete with Tesla, that's the area where you have to do it. Preserving humanity; it's an elevated position.

The famous case study of Kodak's failure to anticipate and respond to digital and mobile-phone cameras is in sharp contrast with Tesla's beautiful example of elevation, but is also interesting for something that has become a less well-known aspect of the company's short-sightedness. When I and other people showed them the new camera-phone technology that was emerging in the early 2000s, Kodak had already secured digital-camera patents and had even launched a digital camera. But it simply did not grasp that the whole basis of its existing film business was going to disappear so swiftly. It is obvious now, as you will also know from reading about how change and disruption work, that Kodak should have stopped perceiving the camera phone as a low threat the very moment when, if not before, the first models were released. Their story might have been very different if that had been their response. However, what is more interesting and important to observe is how its Japanese competitor Fujifilm acted in the face of the very same danger.

Fujifilm went through a process that is most similar to what my company, the Thought Expansion Network, would call an "Unlock Session."[39] Seeing the same data from the camera-phone industries that Kodak had access to, instead of ignoring the potential threat, its executives seemingly decided to elevate up. They chose that response rather than remain limited by the narrow business that Fujifilm and most of its customers would have thought it was working within. It's clear to see that from an elevated perspective, Fujifilm understood that its main thing wasn't just about making cameras. Instead, it was around how *light impacts or damages material.*

Unsurprisingly, Fujifilm had a great deal of technology that was built to work with light and material, because photography is literally "writing with light." So the company's executives asked the group to examine how else it could manipulate the effect that light has on material. From that question, it went on to develop and launch Astalift, one of the world's leading anti-wrinkle skin-care cream brands.[40] Not exactly in the business of cameras, was

81

it?! Now Fujifilm can repeat this with anything. Car tires, roofs of houses, it doesn't matter. Nail polish, clothing, textiles—any material that light damages—its main thing has endless opportunities.

Fujifilm could have elevated its purpose in other ways, of course. It could have declared that it is in the business of making memories, not camera film, and developed products in pursuit of that goal. So could Kodak and, for that matter, Polaroid, whose recent resurgence is based on the premise that the company exists to produce instant, fun memories. That gives it far greater potential for innovation and development. Yet Fujifilm demonstrated a radical elevation that set it apart and gave it a clear advantage over those companies that it would have been competing with prior to the true understanding of its main thing. As this graph illustrates, a lot of companies exist on the left of the picture—they're not elevated. They have a limited view of the business they are in, whereas the business they could *actually* be in is up on the top right, and there are very few companies who elevate to that position.

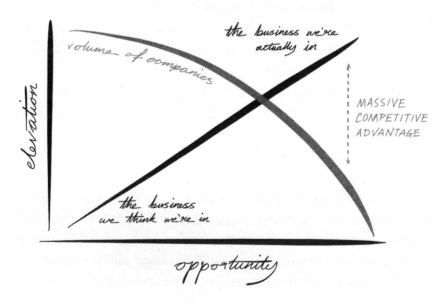

Ultimately, elevation provides an enormous competitive advantage, for this reason:

Our ability to innovate is directly proportional to our ability to elevate.

I'll say it again. The possibilities we have to innovate our offerings are vastly increased when we have elevated to an understanding of our true purpose, skill set, specialism, competency, and in-house knowledge, and therefore have a far greater field of options to consider. The latter parts are more about competency than purpose, but clarity of purpose enables businesses to strive for excellence because they have set parameters on what they are and are not about.

As we're building our blade of Purpose, the first thing that we need to do is to elevate to a position where we can actually see the bigger opportunity more clearly.

Consider how long it took to change a tire in the Indianapolis 500 motor race in the 1950s. Kurtis Kraft, American race-car designer and builder, held the world record for changing a tire during the race, coming in at one minute and six seconds—30 seconds faster than any rival. And that was just to change a single tire. Today, at the time of writing in mid-2017, the record for changing all four tires in a Formula One race is a mere 1.92 seconds. That's how fast things change, and this is not something that is only confined to historic automotive achievements. The speed of change is in fact accelerating. The fact is that the pace of change today is the slowest that you will ever experience.

With that somewhat daunting prospect looming, we need to accept that the mission we currently have in place is not necessarily in tune with the rate of change in the world we are part of. Since Kurtis Kraft's record-breaking achievements, 88% of all automobile companies in the world have gone out of business. Nine in ten of the world's largest companies have disappeared over the same timeframe. Why? Because survival and success are based on our agility and response to change, rather than our size; ironically, size itself can in many cases create most of our risk. The better we get, the slower we move, and the greater the threat becomes.

Think back to the threat that was posed to the traditional music industry by digital downloads, or the risk to telecom companies' lucrative SMS text message revenues presented by the growth of over-the-top internet telecommunications services like WhatsApp. Or consider the battles between wireless and wireline penetration, messaging apps, and social networks, or Hollywood studios and new media producers in China. What's the common link? The fact that the incumbents in all these pan-industry examples demonstrated an alarming lack of response to exponential change, and certainly didn't act with any sense of urgency. The telltale signs of these risks are everywhere. You see the exact same graph that illustrates the difference between a linear growth plan and the reality of exponential change in examples taken from every industry.

The straight line of the figures for Brooklyn taxi pickups against the exponential curved line of Uber rides.

The straight line of department-store sales against the exponential curved line of e-commerce sales.

Even the straight line of validated, mainstream news stories against the exponential curved line of the penetration and acceptance of "fake news" stories on Facebook.

People and businesses alike might be able to avoid reality— but we absolutely cannot avoid the consequences of avoiding reality.[41] To see an opportunity, we need to elevate ourselves outside and above all of the conformity, the way that we think things should be. We need to elevate up and see the whole picture from a different perspective. If Nokia had really been in the business of "connecting people," wouldn't it have naturally created Facebook or something similar? It didn't even try. "Connecting people" turned out to merely be a snappy strapline. The company only thought that it was in the business of selling mobile phones—but that is of course just one of the ways by which people connect. With the ever-blowing winds of change, people are continually finding new means and methods of connection via multiple platforms and devices. Nokia failed because it didn't pour resources into something that it could probably have worked out was going to happen, and the sad news is that this kind of thinking is still dominant. Successful elevation of purpose has to start with management truly believing in that purpose to begin with.

Staying with the example of mobile phones, Mark Zuckerberg, chief executive of Facebook (which doesn't make mobile phones), has already signaled that the end of the smartphone is nigh, likely to be replaced by wearable connected technology such as glasses, watches, and headphones. How many mobile-phone companies are also thinking along these lines and have a product out there that is ready to lead this trend?

There are plenty of other Nokias and Kodaks out there in the world today in every single industry. How many companies are really at the forefront of the stark transformation that artificial intelligence is going to wreak throughout society? We all know it's going to happen. It has even been dubbed the "fourth industrial revolution." But could you name 10 companies that have really ensured their future survival by reorganizing their entire businesses around AI so that they can lead this new era? Incumbent companies are too concerned about their next financial quarters. Artificial intelligence will dominate the world. We know that, we just don't know when it will happen. And in the meantime, shareholders, analysts, customers, and employees want to know about this quarter, next quarter, this year, and next year. It is one of the biggest challenges that all major companies face, and hardly any can claim to have positioned their resources to at best lead the revolution or, at worst, simply survive it.

How to elevate

It is absolutely possible to do this. Look at how Fujifilm coped with the same threat that faced Kodak. This company did not just sit by and let its business disappear because of a trend that it, Kodak, and everybody else could see coming. It survived and thrived by elevating its purpose and realizing that its main thing was not the camera, the film, or the printer business, but about how light damages material. From this elevated perspective, Fujifilm could see that the biggest source of light is the sun, and the biggest material on Earth that is attached to people is their skin. Because this sat squarely within their highest-level "main thing," they also had the knowledge and ability to innovate within this area. It follows as B follows A that it would therefore release its anti-wrinkle skin-cream product, Astalift. That brave, innovative thought process effectively created a brand-new multi-billion-dollar company in the face of change that was on track to decimate its historical core-revenue source.

Thinking like this is rare in business, but it is the best way that any company can try to ensure its survival, because it creates a competitive advantage that is very tricky for others to rival. I am totally convinced that our ability to innovate is directly proportional to our capability to elevate.

So how exactly do you elevate? By following the three-step plan that follows.

STEP ONE: Think how you can describe what it is that your company does without using any of the words that you normally employ.

We have seen how an elevated purpose can be expressed through examples from Google ("Organizing the world's information in an accessible way") to Tesla ("Preserving humanity through sustainable endeavors") and Harley-Davidson ("Enabling the experience of freedom"). You can see that this is about the enabled outcome of what these companies do, rather than the specific activities they undertake.

How would you describe what Airbnb's business raison d'être really is, for example? Even though it was formed when its founders rented out airbeds on their living-room floor to cater to delegates attending a conference in San Francisco where all the hotels were fully booked out, Airbnb is not really in the business of travel and accommodation.

It is in the business of *linking surplus to demand in an incredibly accessible way.*

It should come as no surprise to anybody who elevates their thinking about the company, therefore, that it has now launched Airbnb Music: a music company that links unsigned music tracks to fans of that genre in a brilliantly accessible way. The logic is spot on. If linking surplus to demand accessibly is your thing, then why would you not extend that to any other domain in which a surplus exists?

In the Baltic nation of Estonia, the government's ideology has elevated its function to a main thing of *linking governance to efficiency through capability.* It seems like total common sense when you think about it like that, but not many companies do. Take Kickstarter, for example. This lively, popular, dynamic start-up is not really in the business of crowdfunding. It's in the business of *enabling people to express their belief in something, through the production of it, by providing investment.* What manifestations of this could the company potentially develop from there? There is so much scope! Yet the great irony is that Kickstarter, devoted as it is to getting other people's ideas off the ground, hasn't totally figured this out yet, while Airbnb and the Estonian government have.

Other businesses are catching on. In Japan, the Turtle taxi goes very slowly because it has recognized that pregnant women, careful drivers, and other fearful people don't like driving fast. It has taken a healthy slice of the Japanese taxi market by *linking choice to capability through experience.* Elsewhere, a company in China created baby and cat "clothing" that attaches absorbent mop fabric so that the baby or the cats can clean the floor as they move. Regardless of what you think of the product itself, this is a brilliant example of an elevated focus: in this case, *connecting behavior to purpose through design.* Nothing about mops or cleaning there— and just imagine what else they could create with that elevated viewpoint! In Chicago, Citizen Brick is selling Foxy Blox Club, a set of custom-printed Lego pieces in the form of a play set that features a swinging strip-club scene. It's not to everybody's taste, but what this company is doing is *linking humor to revenue through construction.* Even the crazy trend in Japan for cutting dogs' fur into a square shape around its face demonstrates an elevated position. It is *linking niche interests to reward through competition.*

Are these organizations really elevating their purpose, or are they simply innovating successfully and thereby making themselves more useful, relevant, and more capable of enduring longer? I would argue that the two are almost bound together. Once you have defined your "main thing" as your overriding purpose, then quality, innovation, and creativity can drive excellence in executing it, with far wider-reaching opportunities.

This way of understanding an elevated purpose by observing the main component parts of what exactly it is that a company is doing, and the way it is doing that, will be revisited when we look at the idea of "transposition" in chapter 12.

For now, though, take some time to think about how you could articulate what you or your business does without using any of the words that you normally would. What ultimate outcome are you enabling for your end users through what it is that you do, at the very highest conceptual level?

STEP TWO: Apply what you do to a different industry.

Could you do what you already do in the education industry, for example, but in healthcare or finance? Or could something that currently happens in finance have an application in governance? Could your business model in your industry be used in the area of transport?

As an example, let's look at Airbus. The European rival to Boeing is in the business of commercial flights, so when it patented a modular, self-piloting, flying car early in 2017, it caused some surprise.[42] But looking at this through the lens of an elevated purpose, then it really shouldn't have come as any surprise at all. The logic behind operating commercial flights is figuring out how many people or goods you can fit on a plane, adjusted for costs, fuel, safety, and haulage. Airbus has simply taken what it already has the capability of doing and applied it to the motor industry. The reality is that Airbus has recognized that it is not simply in the business of building equipment to transport people on commercial flights. Airbus's elevated position is as a logistics integrator and engineer that makes it possible for machines to fly. Once the company's elevated purpose is expressed in those terms, the move to make flying cars makes perfect sense.

The Chinese internet wholesale trading giant Alibaba and its chairman Jack Ma have also been able to elevate by applying to a different industry what it is they currently do. They are a good example of a company that demonstrates willingness to change amidst a rapidly changing marketplace. Ma's commercial objective is based on a solution-based approach of fixing problems for people in retailing. Alibaba is now using blockchain technology to limit the amount of counterfeit food that is sold in China. Meat producers can tag their livestock through the company's supply chain so that what is sold to customers is flagged as being authentic and therefore safe to consume. Alibaba needs a high level of quality control for it to be able to generate greater commercial benefit, so Ma has linked quality and service to commercial growth. They have not been constrained by a belief that the company is only able to operate within a certain industry.

How could you apply what you do to a different industry? What is at the heart of your business that would work elsewhere if you simply widened your view?

STEP THREE: If you stopped doing what you do, what problems or gaps would that leave in people's lives?

Regardless of how you feel about the company itself, imagine what a hassle a huge number of people would suddenly have if all Google services were immediately withdrawn and there was no Google search, Gmail, Google Maps, or any of the company's other products and services. In the two decades since the firm was founded, such an occurrence is already unthinkable. Now, ask the same question about your mobile telecoms provider. I suspect the second set of circumstances appears somewhat easier to solve, and you already employ many alternative communication, messaging, and calling services. That is the difference between the long-term sustainability and survivability of a company like Google and that of your phone firm. If I were an operator, that would really concern me.

Has your company found a big enough issue to solve that it makes your offering indispensable, and will ensure your continued relevance and survival because nobody can envisage having to carry on without you being there to help through what it is you do? Is it intrinsic to how everybody lives, or just a "me-too" provider of products or services that could easily be replaced? Most companies are created to fix a particular problem, but are they still fixing it? If times have moved on, what purpose or function is the company now serving? If it doesn't really have a point anymore, then your firm is in trouble. So what *could* it apply its core competencies to that does still solve somebody's mess? (We will look specifically at "mess-finding" as part of building our windmill's third blade.)

Google's purpose is not to provide an email service or even a great search function. Its elevated purpose is "to organize the world's information and make it universally accessible."[43] That is an overarching mission that is difficult even for the cynics to criticize, and the group has now restructured under holding company Alphabet, which can then oversee all the other diverse activities, ranging from driverless cars to its Google X "moonshot technologies" division.

Remember, the question we are asking here is what issue or hole would be left in people's lives if you were to stop doing whatever it is that you currently do. Sadly, when I ask the vast majority of companies this question, they simply shrug their shoulders and reply that customers are fickle and nobody would really care. One firm even told me that the only difference would be that its customers would have to venture a short distance down the road for exactly the same product and service from an alternative supplier. When I suggested that the company's business model had no differentiating merit and was therefore dead, and that it would likely do better by closing everything down and investing in bonds, I was thrown out of the office. A few months later, however, the company announced large-scale closures and job losses, which sadly came as no surprise.

As we conclude this first section of our very first windmill blade, it is useful to remember that elevation drives innovation because innovation is a mindset, not an ideology in its own right. Innovation is mandatory for growth and success, and not just a "take-it-or-leave-it" option for businesses. I like to define innovation as "the ability to change productively for growth." This is because, without innovation, growth is the one thing that is guaranteed not to happen.

In the business landscape, markets do not stay the same, and neither do consumer behaviors or our competitors. As a result, if your company stays the same and does not innovate, it is the only entity in the marketplace that is not changing and therefore not growing. And the innovation of purpose comes through its elevation.

Our ability to innovate is directly proportional to our ability to elevate.

It is a simple progression of strategic thinking and vision, but it involves some leaps of reasoning that many companies and leaders are unable or unwilling to make. I very much hope that isn't the case for you.

CHAPTER SIX

Specification

Once we have elevated to discover our main thing, we need to specify precisely *what our main thing has the purpose of doing.* I have already touched on the "purpose movement" and the popularity of specifying our purpose as the reason why we are here, why we do something, and why it matters. So why is it also so important to clearly specify our purpose in terms of exactly *what* it is that we do? Surely we ought to know this already?

The reason for specification is to communicate the elevated purpose of your company in order to equip it with qualities that enhance its agility and ability to respond to change. It is worth thinking about whether you are doing this with your business. Even if you believe that you are clear about exactly what it is that your business does, I would strongly suggest that you take some time to ensure that its purpose is well-specified, defined, and stated in this way.

There is evidence that clear specification of purpose isn't as common as you might think. According to a Gallup survey in 2015,[44] the percentage of US workers who were fully engaged in their jobs averaged at 32%. The majority (50.8%) of employees were "not engaged," while a further 17.2% were "actively disengaged." If we look at that in terms of productivity and output, there is an actual cost to businesses of $350 billion in the US alone, and in the UK the price we pay is around $35 billion.

One-third of a trillion dollars in America. If this money was being wasted in any other way, there would be a national outcry, particularly when it is cash that could be saved with an executive decision to do something about it. Corporate employee engagement programs are a start, and they have demonstrated clearly that people who have a resonant purpose at work they believe in, as well as a structure they are happy to work within, are more engaged and therefore more productive than those who do not. Companies with such employees have higher output and better staff retention and loyalty.

Why is this so? It turns out that what talented people want has changed. From a requirement in the past based more on high salaries and stable career paths, they now want purposeful work and jobs that fit clearly into the larger context of their career. In other research by PriceWaterhouseCoopers,[45] 60% of chief executives say they don't have the necessary talent within their workforce to derive the most effective results. At the same time, the evidence indicates that those people who are engaged *and* talented are 50% more productive, 33% more profitable, generate 56% higher customer loyalty, and achieve 44% higher customer-retention scores.

This clearly shows that specification of **purpose** plays a critical part in attracting the right talent, and thereby provides better business results. By specifying what our purpose does, we focus managers and employees on key objectives, avoid becoming waylaid by ideas or initiatives that are too niche or sideline projects, and remain alert for opportunities occurring in what we have defined as our "swim lanes." Specification can therefore almost be part of a company's compliance. If an organization is doing something that, on reflection, does not correspond with its stated specified purpose, then that action probably needs to stop.

Online gifting group Notonthehighstreet.com had such a moment when its management realized that, in a quest for revenues and profitability, the group's catalog actually contained a significant number of items that *were* available in conventional bricks and mortar stores. Its immediate response was to stop selling those items, even though that meant its financial results took a short-term hit. One might think that having a specified purpose in the company's very name would have prevented such a mistake. However, the truth is that all organizations can veer off course, and Notonthehighstreet.com deserves praise for spotting this before it got out of control. The company recovered from this episode and has grown substantially. It is also more resilient now to deal with winds of change that might otherwise have damaged its Purpose blade.

Purpose and profitability

The primary measurement used by businesses the world over is that of profitability, so let's examine the part that specification of purpose plays from that perspective. An *average* organization over 11 years has about a 1% profit increase, with a 166% revenue increase, whereas according to Kotter and Heskett,[46] over those same 11 years an *exceptional* organization has a 756% profit increase with a 682% revenue increase. This begs the question, "Why is there such a difference?" The answer, found in the same report, is that an exceptional organization has *"a clearly defined purpose that people believe in."* It's right there in black and white.

Higher-performance organizations display a strong sense of clearly specified purpose through shared values, both internally among employees and also outside the organization among customers, suppliers, and other stakeholders. They have well-defined missions that convey the reason for an organization's existence that inspires others to join the cause. That is exactly why those companies win.

Specify your purpose

In terms of our blade of Purpose, once we have elevated to truly understand the business we are in, we then need to specify exactly what our purpose is as an organization. Following that, the task is then to bring the right people into the organization who have a level of resonance with that specified purpose and can play their part in helping to fulfill it.

In my view, one of the best ways of doing this is to think of the specification technique as a way of finding the best combination of the **holistic** and the **practical.**

Let's return to imagining that you make loft ladders. Then you could think that you're in the loft-ladder business, or that you're in the ladder industry, or that you're in the accessing-lofts market, or even in the house-utilization industry. But what you realize when you have elevated your purpose to find the highest-level answer is that you're in the business of maximizing space. Applying the **holistic** and **practical** methodology, we would first look at our elevated purpose in the most holistic way, which here is all around the maximization of something, in this case space. We then turn to the practical in order to give our purpose focus and direction, and in this example "the maximization of space" could be specified as "maximizing space *in people's homes.*"

The benefit of the specification is that people understand the business that they're really in, and also their role inside that. If you then wanted to execute your elevated, specified purpose in the most practical ways, you can now see that you would be able to get involved with what happens under people's beds, and what happens under floorboards, or what happens inside people's rooms in terms of dimensions, or what you could create with bi-folding doors, and on it goes. Elevation properly defined using specification opens up the opportunities from just being in the loft-ladder industry to absolutely practical ways of maximizing space in people's homes more generally.

Likewise, if you are offering mortgages, you might think you are simply in the business of providing home loans, when what you are really doing is facilitating the human security and independence that people need to further their dreams, whether those involve starting or growing families, making money from investing in the property market, or simply providing better value than the rental market. Once you start to understand what your specified purpose is, you can begin to offer other secured-loan products to your core customers.

Your personal purpose

If you can see how all of this might massively benefit you and your company, but you've never looked at the question of purpose for yourself, then it's a really important starting point.

Identifying personal purpose is important for leaders, as it frames the purpose that they then give to their companies. This is especially true of entrepreneurial businesses, such as Brompton Bicycle, whose entire ethos is structured around the passionate belief in treating people fairly that its chief executive, Will Butler-Adams, discovered on a near-disastrous trip to the Amazon in his early twenties.[47] Having framed and specified his own purpose, Butler-Adams then set about creating a culture of fairness in the business, even when difficult decisions are being taken. This transfers to treating customers fairly, being fair to the company's neighbors in west London, and being responsible with emissions and waste. Although personal purpose and the purpose of a business are separate considerations, they are closely linked when the organization is shaped in the image of its founder or leader.

There are many ways of gaining an understanding of what your personal purpose is. One technique is to find the cross-section between what you love to do, what you are great at (or

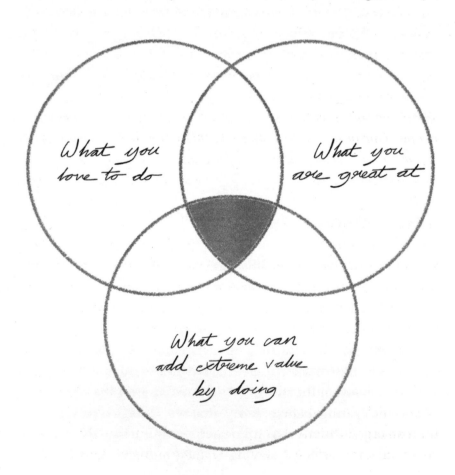

aspiring to be great at), and what you can add extreme value by doing. Where you find the overlap between the three is often a really good starting point if you want to discover your true purpose.

Specifying purpose in business

Of course, this methodology can be applied to businesses too. Operating right within the middle cross-section of these three aspects creates happy environments to work within, and it results in individuals and organizations being very efficient. You can see clear examples of this in companies such as IKEA.

IKEA knows exactly what it is doing and also why it is doing it. That's such a winning combination. Its mission statement says, "*Our vision is to create a better everyday life for the many people. Our business idea supports this vision by offering a wide range of well-designed, functional home furnishing products at prices so low that as many people as possible will be able to afford them.*"

That is the reason why IKEA succeeds. Your mission is what you're enabling as an outcome for the end user. Specify this, and you have established the second section of the Purpose blade, because as I explained at the beginning of this chapter, the reason for specification is to communicate the elevated purpose of your company in order to equip it with all the recommended agility-enhancing qualities. If you are in glassware, for example, you need to specify what it is that you make so that you can explain to customers what the difference is between a glass and a cup.

Specification could be seen as something that might restrict or limit an organization—but this is absolutely not the case, as large companies are perfectly capable of having a single highly elevated purpose that ties together their various activities, or as many elevated purposes as they require, to cover all their myriad operations. Within Google's overarching parent company, Alphabet, for example, Google X is seeking to solve the problems of both cancer and space travel, so these are specifications in those instances, though both fall within the high-level, elevated purpose of organizing the world's information. Neither activity generates any revenue, but fortunately Google's search activity is hugely profitable. And guess what? The search operation has the same overriding umbrella elevated purpose of considering whether it is possible for the world's information to be gathered and presented more effectively. While there may be considerable confusion outside Google about what all the group's different projects are for, and how they make sense under a single corporate umbrella, the understood ethos within the company's campuses is well specified, disseminated, and understood. Specifications of purpose can be split by 15 or 20 different verticals inside a company as long as they all synchronize with the overarching objective.

It is when the purposes of such operations appear to jar with each other that problems can arise. Look at Facebook, for example. It is well known now that the company was set up with far fewer universal societal drivers than those motivations that were more closely connected to Mark Zuckerberg's private life. With critics of the company's web-monitoring operations mounting, the company now has the task of proving to its users what it is actually *for*—a task that it is finding difficult, particularly with teenagers who do not have the same affection for the company as their parents, and who have migrated to rivals such as Snapchat. What does Facebook do exactly, beyond enabling users to stay in touch with their friends—as they now have lots of other ways to do? It is very clear when viewing Google and Facebook side by side which company out of the two has a better-specified purpose.

That has implications for the latter's ability to cope with and adapt to what is coming down the social networks track over the next decade.

That then brings us to the third section of the Purpose blade: integration. This is about making an entire organization understand what it is in the business of, why it does what it does, and why it carries out that function in the way that it chooses.

CHAPTER SEVEN

Integration

What good is a clearly defined purpose of what an organization does, and an ethical, moral, or simply stakeholder-pleasing definition of why it does it, unless those realizations pervade every part of the company? The answer is that a poorly distributed purpose is a purpose of the few, not the many. If it does not resonate with the majority of stakeholders—employees, customers, regulators, and shareholders alike—it stands little chance of spreading in a meaningful way, and its adherents will either lose faith, move on, or do both. Conversely, if your clearly defined purpose does resonate with your people, you can more easily build faith and loyalty, improve staff retention, and increase productivity.

The third part of the Purpose blade is therefore *integration*. This is another term that is generally applied to something different from what I am actually talking about here. Integration is a buzzword in the City for mergers and acquisitions, cutting jobs, improving efficiency, and eradicating costs. And in technology it has come to mean the smooth interaction of technology services on single or combined platforms. Witness the success that Apple has had with its synchronizing of users' experiences across its Mac desktops and laptops, and iPhone, iPad, and iWatch products. That would be an example of how most people generally understand the term "integration".

That's not what I am talking about here, though, which is integration as a vital element in the purpose constituent of what it takes to be agile enough to be permanently ready for perpetual change. What I mean by integration here is how our elevated view of our main thing, once it has been specified into tangible terms that people can understand, is then integrated across the entire organization.

Without this integration of purpose in a way that permeates the whole company, what you end up with is one person who has a vision but no one else who understands or shares that. The challenge that in turn creates is that you end up with total confusion as to the direction that things are going in, across every single constituent part of the organization.

On the other hand, what good looks like is when you find a business that knows exactly what it is they are doing and why they are doing it, and this is understood by every single person, in every single part of the company. One of my favorite examples of this is what the sports brand Under Armour has done.

Under Armour was founded in 1996 by Kevin Plank, a 23-year-old former captain of the University of Maryland American football team. He began the business in the basement of his grandmother's house in Washington DC, traveling up and down America's East Coast with sports clothes in the trunk of his car. His breakthrough came when, tired of having to change out of the sweat-soaked T-shirts he wore under his American football jersey, he noticed that his compression shorts remained dry even during his sports training and practice. This inspired him to make a T-shirt out of a moisture-wicking synthetic fabric, something that competitors Nike, Adidas, and Reebok soon also turned their attention to.

Now Under Armour is a global sports apparel giant, but what I love about the company is that it has absolutely nailed how to build the Purpose blade of a windmill. Consider the following.

The company's vision statement is, *"Empower athletes everywhere."* Its mission statement is, *"Make all athletes better through passion, design, and relentless pursuit of innovation."* Statements of vision, values, and mission are slightly different things, but the implication for our Purpose blade is clear. Here is a company explicitly declaring what it is for, what it aims to achieve, and how it is endeavoring to make its vision a reality.

Under Armour's "four pillars of greatness," meanwhile, are, *"make great product, tell a great story, provide great service, build a great team."*[48] If integration of purpose is truly about ensuring that the goals and very essence of a company pervade every inch of the organization, this is an example of how to ensure that the vision is categorically applied to what the company does, says, facilitates, and develops.

If you take a moment to look further into how exceptionally well their purpose is integrated, then you will also see that they ask everyone in the company to make four pledges,[49] called the four "Wills." This is where Under Armour clearly identifies what is expected from every single member of staff in terms of the way that people think and behave. These pledges are:

I Will—Act like a global citizen.

I Will—Think like an entrepreneur.

I Will—Create like an innovator.

I Will—Perform like a teammate.

The group has precisely defined what "good" looks like, which it then communicates right through the company. It is not separated by organizational charts or office locations. Everyone has clarity and the direction is set. This is how Under Armour has integrated its main thing in practice.

Under Armour's financial records are fascinating, showing a growth of over 2000% in the decade after it floated on the stock market and a profit per employee of around $300,000. This is what the impact of a Purpose blade looks like when it's integrated. Every single member of staff knows exactly what the company does, why it does it, what that means for them, and why they are a part of it. You could ask the receptionist, the cleaner, the chief executive, the chief marketing officer, and the web designer why they're doing what they're doing and they will say, "Well, actually what we're trying to do is empower all athletes everywhere." If you ask, "And how are you doing that?" they'll say, "We do it through passion, design, and innovation." This is true integration of purpose.

Another company in the business of improving performance whose purpose is truly integrated throughout every facet of its operations is McLaren Technology Group, the engineering concern that spans the McLaren Honda Formula One motor-racing team, as well as McLaren Automotive high-performance road sports cars. The truth is that there is not one person from the cleaner to the chef to the chief engineer who is not aware of the fact that they are purely, 100 percent, involved in the business of accelerating performance. That is then seen through every single thing they undertake—from making sure that there is a high-class gym that their staff can access in order to be at their most physical performing ability, to the nutrient-filled food that is served that enables the employees to perform at their best cognitive and physical capabilities. It is seen in the video cameras that are placed over the engineering benches so that if anything goes wrong they can retrospectively go back and find out what happened, which in turn means that performance can be accelerated in the next product iteration. Every single part of the organization has purpose permeating through it, enabling extreme clarity and efficiency.

How to integrate your purpose

Integration is primarily achieved through specification and then well-structured communication that means an elevated purpose can be acted upon and delivered. Disseminating a purpose that pervades every part of a company requires true clarification of message, and the establishment of key points that are *understood when translated into any team*. These steps are equally vital. We can get brilliant clarity, but if we don't construct the story in a way that resonates widely, it won't stick and people won't act.

One issue I am often asked about is whether an elevated purpose can be properly disseminated through a commercial organization—but the reality is that making money and pursuing a genuinely inclusive and engaging purpose do not have to be divergent ambitions. Patagonia, the American outdoor-clothing brand that famously took out an ad urging consumers not to buy the company's products on America's business shopping day of "Black Friday," the day following Thanksgiving Day, is proof of that. The company was primarily created because its mountaineering founder wanted a better quality of necessary gear. But it has shown that a greater purpose—in this case a commitment to conserving the Earth's resources and doing no environmental harm—can operate side-by-side with a healthy profit-and-loss account when everyone throughout the company buys into it and believes in what they are doing. Likewise, The Entertainer, a Dubai voucher-codes company, has the purpose of enabling anyone, everywhere, to have more entertaining experiences. This ethos can almost be smelled at the company's reception desk. It rings true throughout the organization's leadership population and within the ranks of its employees because it is genuine, authentic, consistent, and resonates in everything that a company does.

To build the Purpose blade, all the three sections need to be equally in place. The elevation is the macroeconomic element that is outward-facing enough to see the opportunities for the stated purpose to incorporate other areas. That then requires specification to ensure clarity, and distribution through integration, so that everyone within the company is fully on board. Otherwise, firms that see chances to elevate won't be able to get the right talent to execute those opportunities, or be aligned enough to create the best products or services. Without any process in place, they then go out of business.

It flows from that—and is evidenced by what we see in the financial pages, on the high street, and within the stock market—that there are three main areas in which companies go wrong with building an effective Purpose blade:

- They do not elevate to a position of seeing the business they are truly in. They find it so difficult to break out of marketing myopia and the echo chamber of self-justification that they end up with little external visibility or awareness.

- Even if they have elevated, they are unable to specify that view into an understandable, translatable, extendable way of operating. They may have an instinct about a direction to pursue but they don't know how to define or control it. It's like stepping into a rocket ship with only the experience of riding a horse.

- They fail to spread their elevated purpose across their organization and externally in an understandable way that is highly specified and is something that people can believe in. In its mobile phones heyday, Nokia didn't really want to connect people, despite what its stated purpose said. It was simply interested in shifting handsets. And you cannot properly integrate something that you haven't specified. It just doesn't resonate.

107

I am a big fan of the fact that the "purpose movement" is helping to create a focus on how important it is that a company considers why it is in business and what underlying purpose is driving it on. I also hope that you have a better sense now of how critical it is to also define your purpose in terms of exactly what you are in the business of doing, and pursuing the most elevated version of that. When all of that also begins to resonate through teams, and people throughout an organization become increasingly clear about how the part they play fits within the company's higher-level, well-specified purpose, then that also becomes far more evident and infectious to outsiders—leading to greater benefit and success for everyone.

Integration enhances all the best parts of a company and diminishes the risks of confusion. It is required at this point of our windmill design, because you don't know who the right people are, and you can't get them on board until you've established what the purpose is. Otherwise what you end up with is tens, or hundreds, or thousands of people in the organization, all with multiple different reasons to be involved, but without any useful understanding of what they're involved in. Any execution of the purpose would be disabled or suboptimal due to the level of buy-in from the people involved. If you actually know what business you're in from an elevated perspective, then you can find people who resonate with that purpose, and who are then able to perform, execute, and grow because everyone has true alignment and shares what I call a "belief syntax."

Ultimately the integration of purpose is extremely powerful, provided you have the right individuals within the organization, and this leads us therefore to our second blade: People.

Refresh and review

Your **purpose**, in the context of how to survive in a world of perpetual change, is about **what** your organization essentially **achieves**, rather than **why** it does so. This may require resetting your mindset for a moment from the current purpose movement, which is encouraging companies to set higher values and missions than simply returning profits to shareholders. There is plenty that is laudable about ethical purposes that galvanize and empower staff and inspire loyalty among customers, but they do not guarantee your organization's ability to survive and thrive in a world of perpetual change. That ability is brought instead by an agility of mindset and physical capabilities that enable businesses to switch tack to benefit from forces of change, just as a windmill catches the wind in its sails.

Understanding the "**what**" of your business will enable you to do this without losing sight of what your business is actually all about. On the contrary, it is gaining a genuine understanding of what your company does that will enable it to do this in fresh ways, as trends and circumstances dictate.

This needs to happen in three ways:

- **Elevation**. Think about what it is that your business does. Then think again and try to determine what is the **main thing** that it actually achieves. Try to get to the highest expression of what it is at the meta level that your company is in the business of doing. What exactly are you enabling or creating as the outcome for your customers or users? Ban current products or services from the exercise and get to the nub of what your organization's unique proposition actually is by **elevating** your thinking.

Consider these examples:

Apple does not exist to make the iPad or iPhone. Its elevated purpose is to link industrial design with the creative arts.

Airbnb is not really in the business of travel and accommodation; it's in the business of linking surplus to demand in an incredibly accessible way.

Google does not exist to run search engines. Its elevated purpose is to order and structure the world's information.

Can you describe what it is that your company does without using any of the words that you normally employ? Are you able to apply what you do to a different industry? And what else can you add value by doing if you understand the highest purpose of what your business fundamentally does?

- **Specification.** Once we have elevated to discover our main thing, we need to specify precisely **what our main thing has the purpose of doing**.

Does your business have a clearly defined purpose that people believe in?

Are there shared values among employees, customers, suppliers, and other stakeholders?

Do you have a mission statement that engages and empowers your staff?

What mess would be left in your customers' lives if your business did not exist?

- **Integration** is then about communicating with an entire organization to ensure that it understands what it is for, why it does what it does, and why it carries out that function in the way that it chooses.

Do you clearly identify what is expected from every single member of staff?

*Does everyone in your company understand what "**good**" looks like in the organization?*

Is it clear to all employees why the company is set up in the way that it is, in order to fulfill its purpose?

Is that true in your organization, or are things simply structured as they have always been?

What is the optimal way that your business needs to think and act in order to be able to adapt what products and services it sells, while remaining true to what it is essentially all about?

To build the Purpose blade, all the three sections of elevation, specification, and integration need to be equally in place.

Blade Two
PEOPLE

The way to guarantee that the Purpose blade is properly effective is to ensure that the individuals within the organization are in the best possible shape for the windmill to be operated. So the second blade of our windmill designed to be powered by perpetual change is People. But, just as with the first blade of Purpose, the word "people" needs careful defining.

In recent years, businesses have repeatedly been told by governments, not-for-profit organizations, consultants, engagement specialists, and countless other sources that their most important asset is their people. It has become such a truism that it is now practically meaningless. Since 1991 in the UK, 14,000 organizations have been given the "Investors in People" standard[50] to denote that they have what it takes to lead, support, and manage people well for sustainable results. At the same time, there is a constant flow of news about minimum and living-wage bands, broken supply chains, zero-hours contracts, and other dubious employment practices that suggest that in reality many companies do not invest very much at all in their employees.

The "people" of a company have effectively been seen and used as a public-relations vehicle and marketing technique. Many human-resources directors will confirm privately that people are not prioritized within their organization. There is often widespread concern that productive employees will leave and therefore cost the company money. Employees are not always given attention, provided with personal development opportunities, or helped with their career paths and lives. Companies find it hard to manage people because they essentially view them as forming part of the machinery, rather than the hearts and souls of the organization and the strongest link between what a company does and why it matters.

I do believe that everybody in a company matters and that empowering employees as much as possible is admirable business practice. The definition of "people" that this book is mainly concerned about, however, is around the leaders, managers, and general workers who make decisions that cumulatively dictate whether your company survives and thrives in an age of perpetual change, or dies through an explosive crisis or rapid withering away.

What we are interested in is equipping companies with the wherewithal to adopt flexible mindsets, elevate their purpose, innovate products, and have the most efficient and productive processes to deliver the changes that will be needed in order to succeed. In this context, the imperative is not so much the investment that companies need to pump into their employees, but the need to have the right leadership, management, and shop-floor talent to be able to meet so tall a challenge as that of readying an organization for perpetually changing markets, products, services, and business environments.

This is not a soft, fluffy subject.

The Association of Insolvency and Restructuring Advisors has calculated[51] that, out of a cross-section of companies of all shapes and sizes, 52% of businesses go bankrupt primarily because of "internal triggers"—meaning those in-house issues that the management has decided in favor of or against, and tried to execute accordingly. Another 15% go bust due to "external triggers"—those things that happen outside the company that management doesn't do anything about. 24% of firms sink due to a combination of those internal and external factors that management don't do anything about, 8% fail because of events beyond their control, and only 1% die simply due to what could only be attributed to pure bad luck.

That's what is happening to the companies all around us, all the time. The only thing that should surprise us about this research is that we are not more worried, anxious, or downright paranoid about it happening to us.

What this means, alarmingly, is that 91% of the reasons that these companies went out of business is down to the way that *people inside an organization* have reacted or failed to respond to the various stimuli that ended up destroying their firms. While advice that business success is "all about the people" can become a simplistic platitude, it is crucial for organizations to be aware of and pay attention to the outcomes of their leaders and employees making poor decisions.

Even when purpose, elevation, and integration are understood and companies are inspired about which opportunities to pursue, something often holds them back from taking the required steps toward designing their business for perpetual success in an environment where their very existence will otherwise ultimately be under threat.

This "something" is more often than not our organizational structures and the way we're set up to do business. Organizations can cage their people inside structures, and sometimes companies find themselves in structural situations that are not conducive to them growing. At other times, there are rational fears that we know we can overcome with a volume of understanding that's greater than our level of fear. But uncertainty is also a major restraint. Companies wait for concrete facts and statistics before making decisions, and before the facts arrive all they have are forecasts, scenarios, and projections, on which they are reluctant to actually make judgments.

To get to corporate willingness, companies have to meet and defeat another paradox, which is that change is the enemy of the competent. When things are going well, and people feel that they are doing a good job and generating results, then change is the last thing in the world that they want to confront. When this idea is married with the reality that I will reiterate once again—that today's change is happening at the slowest pace that we will ever experience—the result is that those businesses that are the most competent and among the best at what they do will often find it harder than others to realize that when the winds of change blow, they have the choice to build a wall or a windmill. As you now know, the benefit has to outweigh the cost of changing, but also, so importantly, the cost of staying the same or not changing. It is this latter cost that is often the hardest to calculate. If companies are to build windmills, not walls, they need to change the points of reference around which they make corporate decisions. As I suggested in part 1, rather than view every decision through the lens of return on investment (ROI), we need to continually keep in mind a different definition of the same acronym—the risk of inaction. A failure to make a decision is, after all, a kind of decision in itself. Inaction stultifies people and lulls them into that false sense of security that is the belief that their position and that of their employer enjoys some degree of permanence. I am not a believer in creating organizational tension for its own sake, but a company's people do need to understand the importance of being in a constant state of readiness for change.

Builders of walls look at return on investment by itself. Windmill-builders, however, will also assess the risk of doing nothing at all. Unfortunately, many companies I've observed have a huge number of barriers in place. Many people are in organizations where it's hard to get things done because of structures that are suboptimal. There is also often a big confusion between what it means to be a boss and what it means to be a leader. These are two very different things.

I am of the impression that people get into leadership positions in one of three ways.

The first is extremely common, which is a political ambition to be in charge. Not necessarily because they are good at being in charge, or because they should indeed be in charge, but because they simply want to be in charge. And so they will manipulate circumstances in order to achieve this.

There is a second route that is based on a form of worth-based meritocracy. You create great things, you hit targets, you achieve results, you rise to the top, and you're promoted.

The third way is that of accidental leadership—for example when someone resigns and you end up being Prime Minister of the country, or the new Director or MD.

There are different ways of getting there. But when you are there, the difference between a boss and a leader—or to put it a better way, an ineffective leader versus an effective leader—is that an effective leader is someone who stands in front of the team when they are losing and represents the cause. And when— or if—success happens, they stand behind the team and allow the team to shine. We find the opposite contrast with an ineffective leader. So when things aren't going so well, an ineffective leader pushes the team forward, focusing on blame, which then leads to attrition. When things go right, the ineffective leader takes all the credit.

What I find the most paradoxically confusing, and have been unable to answer over time, is how for some reason some people are able to be an ineffective leader yet still achieve financial gain and business merit. I fail to understand how we can still observe so many leaders who are self-serving, blatantly without the faith of their staff, acting in evident contrast to the four blades of the "Windmill Theory"—yet who are still rewarded with the highest praise.

We know, being reasonable people, that a person who says that something cannot be done should definitely get out of the way or certainly not interrupt an individual who's actually undertaking that very task. Nonetheless, when we look at our People blade, we see that there is a great deal of fear, uncertainty, and misplaced comfort. We need to address those three barriers and understand how we can move beyond fear, uncertainty, and comfort in various different ways.

The first barrier to surpass is fear. In *Risk: The Science and Politics of Fear*,[52] Dan Gardner discusses how our level of fear is inversely proportional to our level of understanding. However,

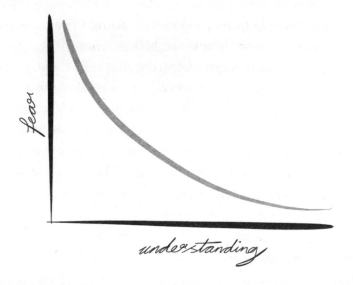

this is only true in terms of rational fear. Irrational fear doesn't work like that. Irrational fear is not linked to a level of understanding. You could inform someone with a fear of flying that the most dangerous part of an airplane journey is the drive to the airport, which is true. You can even try and convince someone that only one in five million airline journeys involves a fatality, contrasting heavily with the one in 35,000 motor traffic journeys that causes deaths.[53] However, if their fear is irrational, even an addition of understanding won't necessarily be enough to change their level of fear.

In business, irrational fear is something that can be seen either as a hindrance or an irrelevance. If it's a hindrance, then the test will be one of willingness, and we will address that shortly in the first section of the People blade. What we do know is that when fear is rational, the level of understanding we have decreases the amount of fear we feel. This means that to actually eliminate fear, the first port of call is to raise the level of understanding in organizations, and enable people to actually grasp exactly what's going on.

There's only one exception to this, and that is in the circumstance where people have a high level of understanding but yet they're still very fearful. In my opinion that means they probably have a good, rational reason to be fearful and they should be listened to. Sometimes people who are fearful despite a great deal of understanding are simply called wise.

The second barrier is uncertainty. In cases of uncertainty what we need to do is attempt to decrease the level of uncertainty by reducing the level of complexity. As much as fear and understanding are inversely proportional, uncertainty and complexity are directly proportional. Many people who are very uncertain are that way because they see a hugely complex set of speculative outcomes. What we need to be doing in these situations is taking the time to explore a number of very different scenarios and projections, then make the predictions that are actually based on those. In that way, we can gradually base our predictions more and more on as many established facts as we can. Ideally we need to be continually diminishing the level of complexity, and thereby the level of uncertainty. This is an extremely effective method for overcoming the barrier of uncertainty.

Fear and uncertainty, however, are minor inconveniences in comparison with getting people out of their comfort zones, which can be one of the biggest barriers to overcome if we really want to be effectively powered by change.

This is the hardest thing to overcome in anyone. The reason it's the hardest is because our human condition is to naturally try to find comfort. We resist any change that pulls us away from that comfort in most cases, even when shown that the magic happens far away from where our comfort zone tends to be. But the underlying concept beneath that of comfort is actually the idea of our *willingness*, or lack thereof, and it is this idea of will that I want to address in the first section of our People blade.

Over the next three chapters you will see that the essential sections of the People blade are therefore about the skills that are required to adapt to change and people's willingness to do so, the importance of a concept I call "productive paranoia" in leadership, and how we can find the best ways to manage the paradox of exploiting our existing business assets while exploring new opportunities.

But let's start with this idea of willingness to change, respond, and adapt.

CHAPTER EIGHT
Skill and Will

There is no shortage of examples of companies that lost their way because their people were not up to the task of making the decisions they needed to make in order to adapt to change.

The truth is that a paradox exists, expressed by the idea that change is the enemy of the competent; the more successful we become, the more of a disadvantage we carry in terms of our ability to succeed in the future. Success seduces all of us into thinking that we cannot possibly lose. And the short-termism of the financial markets creates a powerful disincentive for any change that does not immediately enhance the bottom line.

Consider this quote from Stephen Elop of Nokia, the Finnish company whose mobile phones were ubiquitous in the 1990s and early 2000s. He was chief executive during the period that it suffered a dramatic loss of its share in the market that it had previously dominated.

"We didn't do a thing wrong," he says,[54] "but somehow we lost. We understood the problem but at some deep level we couldn't accept what was happening. Many big projects just carried on. We examined the sales projections for the following quarter when our eyes should have been focused much further ahead."

He continues, "The worst thing that can happen to a company is to run out of money and be forced into bankruptcy. Enormous success is perhaps the next-worst."

This section of the People blade therefore is about the ability of you and your leadership to identify opportunities for the business to grow and to *ensure that the willingness and processes that will actually make those changes happen are in place.* I call this "skill and will." It is about how your company goes about getting inspiration for opportunities once it has elevated its purpose and views the business arena with a clear understanding of its "main thing," and how it then executes upon those opportunities.

This is where we start our journey of exploring why the People blade is so critical to the ability of an organization to adapt to and be powered by perpetual change. It concerns the fact that it is our emotional and intellectual decision-making criteria that determine how we respond to external stimuli. A large part of it is about leadership, but it then percolates down through the board, executive management team, vice presidents, regional directors, and operational managers, right down to the shop- and factory-floor operatives (in the same way that we have seen when looking at true integration of Purpose within that blade). The old expression that "a fish rots from the head" is extremely apt here. If your company has misaligned leadership, it doesn't matter how fantastic your junior salesperson is. The business is not being guided in the right direction.

Willingness to change is critical

The following case studies are examples of what happens when something goes wrong within the People blade of the Windmill Theory. Even though there is also evidence within these stories of how an elevated, well-specified, and integrated purpose could have played a part in changing the companies' fortunes, this is very much a point about people—and specifically about their *willingness*. A willingness to consider the prevailing winds of change. A willingness to have more robust internal and external lines of enquiry.

Nokia had some truly outstanding staff and managers, but the decisions that were made at the top table were poor, just like those at the Blockbuster video chain. Kodak, meanwhile, had most of the patents that existed for digital cameras in the late 1990s but ended up being floored by the move toward digital, rather than actually leading the change as they so rightfully could have done. What upended these companies were not decisions made by middle or junior executives; they came right from the most senior directors who refused to use change as a powering mechanism, viewing it instead as an enemy. In some cases, they were simply not willing to take the risk of making any fundamental change. In others, such as Kodak's, the company did not have a process to effectively execute the change that they knew was needed. The role of the Process blade and the way that it is linked to the willingness of leaders to change will be examined in more detail in chapters 14 to 16.

Other examples of companies that were floored by poor judgments in the boardroom include smartphones pioneer BlackBerry, early social network darling MySpace, retailers C&A, BHS, and Woolworths, and sports shoemaker Reebok, as well as most of the old, traditional music companies and also a good many independent film-production companies. In fact, it is extremely difficult to find examples of companies that have failed that have not been cursed by bad top-down decisions that accelerated their demise. Usually, these poor decisions relate to holding a view of change as an enemy to resist, rather than a powering mechanism.

BlackBerry was too dogmatic in its refusal to embrace or copy the Apple or Android operating systems, until it was too late. MySpace refused to believe that customers' tolerance of advertising on its sites was decreasing and was so focused on monetizing its viewing "eyeballs" that it overfilled its platform with advertising to satisfy its stakeholders. Woolworths, BHS, and C&A never took their operations online, choosing to double down instead on offline retail in physical stores. Reebok, meanwhile, had an early lead in the sports clothing market but did not realize that fashion is not simply about apparel; it is also heavily influenced by technology and experience. The music industry, meanwhile, was blinded to the threat of failure by the soaraway success that compact discs had experienced in disrupting the decades-old technology of vinyl records. Compared with 7- and 12-inch records, a CD was hard to damage, took up less space in bedrooms and front rooms, held more content, was easier to manufacture, and even ended up selling at about the same price or more. What could possibly go wrong?

At these firms, it was all too apparent that the technology or the environment had changed, and the facets of the business that drove its historical success in the past were not going to be able to do that anymore. At record stores chain HMV, for example, the writing was on the wall for the company way before it went into administration in 2013. The CDs and DVDs that the store was selling had long been replaced by digital downloads and file streaming. Ventures to fight this well-forecast development had included devoting whole floors of their shops to gadgetry and games in an attempt to attract teenagers and other music fans. At almost every half-year results announcement, the company unveiled a new initiative, product area, or sales pitch, akin to putting another brick in its wall, that was designed to halt the slide. None of those activities enabled the company to stay afloat, though another smaller business was formed with the purchase of HMV assets from the administrators and still trades today.

HMV should have asked itself the question about how it could realistically continue to run a physical and retail business when those two modes of operating were going to be severely threatened. Instead, the company announced that it was going to improve its physical retail proposition. It was commercial suicide and it was voted on and agreed by the company's very topmost senior management. This is why a company's People—and let's not forget this also includes those in leadership—are the second blade of the windmill that enables businesses to thrive and succeed in the face of perpetual change.

Like Nokia, however, HMV made a critical mistake. The group saw the changes that were happening in the music and technology industries, and in the consumer environment, but it chose to ignore the necessity for structural evolutions, investing instead into what amounted to superficial, tactical amelioration. Starting to sell headphones and tablet computers, and to invite live bands in to perform in stores, were all tactics that were never going to add more than marginal value, compared with the destruction to the company's basic operating model wrought by the Internet and the associated changes that brought.

A more fundamental strategic decision would have involved deliberating over how the company could operate in a digital environment where ownership of recorded assets was going to be much less important than it had been in the past. HMV could have set up something like the Spotify music-streaming service. It had the opportunity to construct an effective rival to iTunes before iTunes was launched. It also had options to create a record label, from a music distribution company, package and sell digital rights, or perhaps launch music-tuition businesses. Maybe it could even have created MTV before that operation was formed. HMV had all of these potential opportunities on the table, and all of them were supported in a positive way by the latest demographic trends and market research. The company also had in its favor worldwide fame, a venerable history and name, and enviable retail distribution networks. Yet it chose to ignore the dominant, driving trends of its sector and to focus instead on marginal gains that might save the next quarter from being as bad as it would otherwise turn out to be, but that were never going to rescue the company from its plunge into insolvency, or reverse its decline.

Why did it make this choice? Because the purpose of HMV was to monetize the physical retail of products. It was wedded to the idea of selling physical products in bricks and mortar stores when all of the evidence was that the future was going to be digital, not physical, and sales were going online. Now the trend has progressed even further, to the point that the retail construct of purchasing music is moving far more toward transient rental, just like what's happening to buying motor cars and booking taxis. The signposts were clear enough. Ownership was becoming a thing of the past; physical products were going to be digitized. I recall speaking to the company about these trends in 2000 and 2001 when I was chairman of the British Music Industries Association. The company's response was that it had a view of the next 10 to 20 years that very much involved physical retail and in particular CDs and peripherals. They accepted that the trends I was talking about could well create a very different future in 20–30 years' time. However, it would take until then for it to take hold and HMV's brand strength would enable the company to respond quickly when the new future took effect. (Recognize any business poisons here?!) The irony was that I was not speaking about the future but about the present. The problem with the future is that it starts happening now, and everything I was talking about at the time was already occurring.

Leadership, tone, and direction

Leadership sets the tone and direction of a company. The first action that a new chief executive often announces is to change the personnel in the key positions reporting directly to him or her. Sadly, this frequently results in leadership structures being realigned in a way that protects the CEO, rather than recruiting the best brains and operational know-how to steer businesses through all the tricky issues that they have to continually navigate.

Instead, if a company's elevated purpose is properly in place and fully integrated right through the bloodstream of an organization, then this is the most effective way to get the right leaders involved. Businesses can have the world's best engineers and marketers, but if employees further down the scale do not understand the link between what they're doing and why it matters, organizations end up with huge inefficiencies. Their people are not aligned with the group objectives, and the frontline staff end up being disconnected and listless wage slaves who work to their strict hours, doing as little as possible within that time. That is when companies' sick days increase, workflows plummet, and the most talented people jump ship because they cannot progress their ambitions at such an outfit.

If you want to see which companies are suffering from this kind of malaise, correlate the firms suffering sudden outflows of talent or seeing an increase in the number of their employees posting their resumes on LinkedIn. Take this statement from Jeff Jones, who quit as president of Uber in March 2017 and is one of a number of senior executives to suddenly depart the company.

"It is now clear . . . that the beliefs and approach to leadership that have guided my career are inconsistent with what I saw and experienced at Uber and I can no longer serve as president of the ride-sharing business," he said.[55] Jones was a major hire for Uber when he was attracted from US department stores group Target, where he had been the company's well-regarded chief marketing officer. He was given the task of remaking the ride-sharing group's pioneering image after a series of controversies, including allegations of abrasive management and allegations of sexism and sexual harassment. But he left because he could not stomach the misalignment of purpose that his company had been exhibiting.

You will not find many absolute binary statements in this book, because I believe in chaos theory, unpredictability, and I am not a stoic. But here is one: when there is a misalignment of purpose within an organization, the most talented people always leave. And after that happens, the people who are left behind do not tend to work as well as before.

So how can this be fixed? Well, the overarching answer is about the willingness that people have to embrace change, as well as their willingness to constantly improve their ability to use that change as an empowering force, rather than view it as an enemy to perpetually fight against and resist. I can assure you that this is absolutely not about platitudes; it is rather a methodological approach to viewing and using change. And by change, you will know by now that I mean that every company in the world needs to accept that change is the only constant, and that they therefore have to structure the way that they view leadership, the make-up of the organization, and its decision-making to be harmonious with—and indeed powered by—that change.

There is a difference between telling your employees that they have to accept change, and constructing strategies, behaviors, staff contracts, and innovation approaches based on those changes. These are mindsets that are as contrasting as those of regarding purpose as your reason for being or seeing it as being about your belief in an aspirational goal. When a lot of managers

129

tell the teams within their organizations that things are going to change, what they mean is that the changes have been agreed already, are going to happen, and if people don't like them then they will have to leave. That is not the kind of empowering, purpose-led response to change that I am talking about here, and the People blade is definitely not about that kind of management.

Three-year plans cannot be the answer in a world where change comes so fast that they constantly risk by their very nature being at least six months out of date. This is a challenge because there is also a need to set the expectations of the stock market and to win the hearts and minds of investors, as well as their pockets. The last thing you want is for shareholders to sell your stock halfway through your plan because they cannot see where the company is going, and therefore no longer have the confidence to hold its stock. Stock-market analysts nowadays increasingly want to see in a company's leadership the flexibility, adaptability, and willingness to be able to move in an agile fashion, according to where the opportunities and risks present themselves.

Reflect for a moment on whether you have processes in place that demonstrate your company's willingness to be responsive to change.

One good indicator is often the innovation and development timeframe of a company. At Nokia, for example, this was set at 18–24 months. Even if the company's management had seen the changes that were on the way, made the right calls, and selected the very best responses, the shortest period that it took to bring something to market was one and a half years down the road. Having a process like this, given everything we know about the pace of change, is now commercial suicide.

Apple's approach, meanwhile, is to develop what is technologically possible and then build backwards to what the company believes is capable of being marketed adroitly to a mass audience. It is well known, for example, that the iPad was actually devised and created before the iPod. The two products arrived on the market in the opposite order, of course, but this was because Apple reversed what was possible technologically into what was marketable in the day and age of the time. Apple's responsiveness to change is not based on looking at what is happening in the market and then worrying about how to construct what it is doing in response. Its approach is to bring forward ideas and products that the group has already innovated, depending on the market demand. Apple looks more at market-demand changes in its innovation and design development timeframes than it does at the actual technology itself. So when customers are buying more tablets and fewer laptops, its product launches adapt to that trend accordingly. It is a great example of corporate responsiveness to market demand. Competitor moves and market share are less important to Apple than commercial growth and per-unit profit.

Yet Apple is not necessarily making itself resilient or future proof against winds of change by using this approach. By defining its purpose almost entirely in commercial terms, it mobilizes its resources in the direction of amassing enormous commercial resources, such as its large cash stockpile. Decide for yourself: in the next five years, is Apple likely to hire the world's most visionary designers, and recruit the most maverick innovators and product developers? Or is it more likely to focus more on increasing its $60 billion cash pile? And will that cash mountain last the company more than 10, 20, or 30 years? Is Apple really building to last? Or are they building to win now? Is there a difference between what Steve Jobs's vision for the company and executed purpose would be now, and that of Tim Cook, his successor as chief executive? Is there a clue in the number of senior executives who have been departing Apple over the past 18 months?

Visionary thinkers get nervous and unsettled when they see that their companies are realigning their purpose from one of putting a dent in the universe through the intersection of creative arts with industrial design, to something more commercial and volume-driven. Perhaps most importantly, do the people who are leading and working within Apple really display a willingness to change, even when that is uncomfortable or costs the company revenue in the short term?

A stationary stationer?

People-based questions can also be asked when we consider the sustainability of Britain's most famous and historic news and stationery chain: WH Smith. Regular visitors to the stores will be familiar with the way that the company has cut costs, reduced staff numbers in the shops, encouraged customers to use self-check-out machines rather than those few desks that are still manned by a person, and introduced snaking lines that make purchasers queue for longer than would otherwise be necessary, pinned in by shelves teeming with impulse purchases. It is a strategy that has seen the company make a great financial recovery from the days when it was involved in so many areas, from garden products to DIY, that people did not know what it was for anymore. But it is also a risky approach because it opens up an opportunity for a new rival to come in and take market share. Imagine the entrance of a competitor that removed queues, kept prices low, and enabled customers to access the products and services that they desire in an efficient way, all within a retail environment that they can believe in.

Taking WH Smith down the strategic route it has embarked on was a management decision—one made by the company's top people—and has produced impressive short-term financial results. However, the further that an organization moves itself away from consumers' beliefs and desires, the more open you are to having your business taken away by a competitor that actually notices and listens to what customers want.

Sales at the motor side of Tesla experienced a double-digit increase in 2016–17, while there was a decrease in the overall sales of the general car industry. Why did this happen? Because customers believe in what Tesla is trying to do, which is to save the planet by reducing carbon emissions. Consumers have a keen nose for whether a company is truly willing to do what it takes to walk the talk of its purpose and ambition. And a company's people who believe it too are powerful brand leaders and ambassadors.

People, purpose, and decision-making

There is a purpose-based challenge that manifests itself within an organization's people and reaches into their decision-making and staff behavior, which in turn filters down to change consumers' perception and has a knock-on negative commercial effect.

Do Toyota drivers have a similar belief in that company? Are teenagers who are using Snapchat more than Facebook flagging a problem down the line for Facebook chief executive Mark Zuckerberg? Is there a reason why hundreds of companies pulled advertising from Alphabet's YouTube in 2017 in response to the extremist messages they saw being broadcast on the company's channels? In mobile phones, consumers are swiftly moving on from the joy that they used to experience when unwrapping their new devices to frustration that they have to constantly buy new adapters and associated products and subscriptions. Teenagers are spotting this misalignment between their own purposes and those of the phone manufacturers—and they are taking their purchasing habits elsewhere. Something has gone wrong at these companies.

In the UK, The John Lewis Partnership has long operated such a link with its "never knowingly undersold" mantra and its investment in product quality and customer service. At Virgin Group and also at Patagonia, we can again see the link between quality of service, quality control, and commercial growth, fixing problems in the supply chain so that customers do not feel exploited and therefore logically want to bring their custom to these suppliers. The staff of all three organizations resonate their core values and beliefs. One has only to ask in the store where a certain item is on the shelves of Waitrose, or how to care for Patagonia mountaineering equipment, to find knowledgeable and helpful staff who believe in their companies, and who have the will and skill to change their way of operating if they are required to do so.

Would WH Smith think about fixing quality-control issues in the general retail supply chain? It's a question of its willingness to change, and the answer that is given to that question will determine whether companies can survive the winds that are going to be blowing them and their competitors around in the marketplace over the coming decades.

There are three important lessons when it comes to promoting and encouraging the development of skill and will in an organization.

1. Develop a process that never stops testing your assumptions.

How often do you, your leadership team, and decision-makers test your assumptions about what your business is capable of, what it is going to achieve, and in which ways it can be stretched? Weekly, monthly, annually, or not at all? Do you view the world from an absolute framework of bias or are you genuinely open to being challenged, tested, and probed? Even if your assumptions about your business were tested and found to be appropriate a month ago, do they still pass that test today?

2. **Create a plan that accesses and harnesses new thinking from all people both inside and outside your organization.** Nobody wants to end up with the type of iPhone that Tim Cook says Apple would have ended up with if it had listened to all its critics. But are you actually listening to the people whose ideas and opinions count? If I had solicited the right advice and listened to what people were saying about Mydeo, the video-streaming company I worked for after my TV channel disaster, I am sure that somebody would have told me that YouTube was about to make my offering outdated and superfluous.

3. **Have a strategy for the 98%.** I find it very helpful to pretty much assume that there is 1% of information we know that we know, and another 1% of things we know that we don't know. The remaining 98% comprises all those thoughts, ideas, trends, innovations, evolutions, and realities *that we don't know that we don't know*. What is your strategy for tapping into this 98%?

Getting out of the comfort zone

In the introduction to this People blade, I suggested that of the barriers we need to overcome, getting people out of their comfort zones is one that critically needs to be addressed in order to be effectively powered by change. Of course, we can try to tackle that by experimenting with things that don't make us comfortable, but underlying that is whether we're even willing to give those things a go. When it comes to willingness, the drive comes from either an innate or a learned behavior that means we are prepared to take risks and chances. The willingness to try also brings with it an optimism that there may be a better potential future, uncovered through this experimental streak that views taking chances as a way for people to learn. There is an element of boldness in willingness, but also one of risk. This is vital because, without that will, the chance to be able to use change productively is minimal, if not non-existent.

For me, the presence of real will is so important in how I then deal with the people I come across in life and business, I plot everyone I meet on my Personality Assessment Matrix, which is illustrated below:

The Personality Assessment Matrix

	Will	No Will
Skill	Lead	Align
No Skill	Learn	Avoid

There's will or no will, skill or no skill. The people with no skill and no will obviously shouldn't be around us, they shouldn't be hired by us, and you definitely shouldn't work for them. I cannot emphasize enough how strongly I use the word "avoid" here to define this category. On the other hand, people with will and skill, at the top left, are evidently leaders. So you've got those who should be avoided at all costs, and those who absolutely should lead. It's rare to find people who demonstrate both will and skill but are not already in leadership positions, because they tend to be natural leaders. They rise to the top, they fight to the top, they arrive at the top, they buy themselves into the top, they earn their way into the top. Any way around, they find a way of doing it. If in the unlikely event you do identify people who have both the will and the skill, but are not yet in a position where they can lead, then do everything in your power to get them leading, and fast.

The most common mixes are where we find people either with will but no skill, and/or people with no will but with some skill. Those who have no will, but yet possess the skill, are where the largest challenges lie. The people with the will but no skill are actually the lowest of the challenges, because even if skill is absent or lacking, that can be taught when the will is in place. These people can learn.

So where will is present we have those who can lead or those who need to learn, and we've also identified those with neither skill nor will who we must avoid at all costs. That leaves us then with the people who probably could do stuff, as they have the skill, but without any will they just couldn't care less about doing it. This is where you find the people in your organization who are "actively disengaged."

The only option here is to find a way to align, in an attempt to increase their level of will. Throughout my career I've observed and tried many techniques to enable those without the will to actually care, and from all those experiences I've come to realize that there are five steps of working with, and trying to align with, these people:

1. Establish the most understandable way of communicating your mission, but keep that to yourself until point 3.

2. Speak with them about what resonates with them in their life.

3. See where there is potential overlap for your company mission to empower their personal desires.

4. See where there is potential overlap for their personal desires to fuel your company mission.

5. If there is no alignment possible, attempt to learn from them as much as possible. Everyone has insight if given permission to share.

Ultimately the people with the will—no matter their skill—are those who actually go on to build the windmill. What the windmill requires, generally, is an ability to test, learn, and improve; test, learn, and improve; test, learn, and improve, repeatedly. No one would even bother trying to test, learn, and improve unless they have the will to do so, which is why this part of the blade is so incredibly important.

Skill and will is the first step of designing the People blade. Without this, nothing else can happen. This is a critical path. Will is required to operate not only this blade but the other blades too, in order to drive toward business success in the face of those winds of perpetual change.

Take the example of a Ukrainian guy called Max. This is his start-up career in his own words: "My first company failed with a great bang, the second one failed with a little bit less, but still failed. The third one, you know, proper failed, but it was kind of okay. I recovered quickly. Number four almost didn't fail. It still didn't feel really great, but I did okay. Number five was PayPal."

This man is Max Levchin, and that fifth company, which he co-founded with Peter Thiel and two others, became a financial technology pioneer that merged with Elon Musk's X.com in 2000, was floated on the stock market, and was later bought by eBay for $1.5 billion. Now PayPal, which is an independent company again, is valued at $61 billion on Nasdaq, and Levchin has a net worth of more than $300 million. Levchin had, and still has, the willingness to test, learn, and improve. This is the spirit of the people you need for your windmill and in your organization.

When people look at Levchin now, they think of PayPal and get jealous, believing that he somehow lucked out. What they don't necessarily know is that before PayPal his four previous firms ended up being tremendous financial disasters. What kept him going in pursuit of his dream? His objective, and elevated purpose, was not to make a great deal of money. It was to bring to market ideas and businesses that solve problems in innovative ways. I am always impressed by the mindset of people who continue to put all their efforts into something, even when they know that the odds are stacked against them.

There are lots of people like Levchin who just keep on going, even if most of them do not achieve the level of financial or industry success that he eventually had. However, there are even more individuals who make one or two attempts and then simply give up. Many people become victims at this point, thinking there is nothing they can do about their plight. From my perspective, from the first three hours of my very first day at school, my experience of being bullied significantly meant that I found very quickly in my life that I had to make a decision about whether I wanted to try to survive or whether I should just fold into being a victim. I initially made the wrong choice, but 11 years later I was ready, and had the willingness, to go in a different direction.

Just as it was possible to glimpse the future of the music industry back in 2001—not by being a futurist but because the changes had already started to happen in that year—some of the trends that will dominate the next 20 years are already apparent. Artificial intelligence is already being proclaimed as the fourth industrial revolution. Ford has announced that driverless cars will be on our roads by 2020, while one-third of London's taxis are forecast to be driverless by 2022. Enormous change is coming in these areas. Everybody knows it. It is just a question of when it really arrives and who is leading the charge. But we are tempted to ignore it because of our own career plans, or upcoming retirement, or because of a strategy culture that measures everything on linear spreadsheets.

An exponentially increasing rate of change requires us instead to have an accelerating plan that quickens its pace as the years roll on. Refer back for a moment to the graph in chapter 3 that illustrates the risk (or opportunity) within that delta of disruption. The rate of change is like a hockey stick, so you need to create a business plan that accelerates inside itself in an unpredictable way. You will not find that on the curriculum at Harvard Business School, Insead, or any other of the world's top business universities, because there is not a nice, easy, standard formula for that. It is not based on a mathematical plan but on the realization of a purpose, the positioning of the right people who are aligned with that purpose, and the development of flexible products that fit the context of the time. And all of that requires a set of processes that are porous, allowing input from the outside and regeneration on the inside. This is the "formula" for an accelerated plan. To even begin to achieve these things, however, requires a huge amount of will.

At IKEA Group, Jesper Brodin understands this. He is most definitely an example of someone in the "lead" box with huge quantities of both skill and will. He views this cycle of uncertainty as a major opportunity for his company. He knows that consumers' frustrations with having to put together the company's furniture has got to the point where it is starting to limit the company's values to deliver a better life at home for its customers. IKEA's main focus nowadays has switched to creating modular furniture that can snap into shape, so that the experience of self-construction is much better. In IKEA's mindset, that turnaround could not happen gradually over 10 or so years. It had to become a reality much, much faster, because it could see that the problem it needed to fix was here now and threatening to grow.

Just as the world changed a couple of decades ago with concerns about the environment and climate change meaning that furniture had to be recyclable and originate from sustainable sources, the zeitgeist of customer frustration was developing so rapidly that IKEA had to act at once and spread the word.

There are also a fair number of companies who do understand that the most successful businesses need to constantly find the willingness to reinvent themselves. Alibaba, Virgin Group, Amazon, and Patagonia all do exactly that. Decades ago when Jack Welch was running General Electric, then the world's largest company, he argued that if the rate of change is faster outside an organization than inside it, the business is already dead—it is just a matter of time. Welch's several thousand percent growth of GE during his time in charge was based on continual innovation of the company and never resting on its laurels. And that is what willingness looks like in practice.

Our willingness to change is the greatest ability that leaders, managers, and regular workers can bring to their employers. It is a vital component in the People blade of our windmill of perpetual change.

CHAPTER NINE

Productive Paranoia

Alongside willingness, we need something that I call "productive paranoia," the second section of our People blade. Productive Paranoia is one of my favorite subjects of all time, because amongst the compliments I am honored to receive from speaking on stage, there's a contingent of people who say that I've scared them in some way into taking action. It was enlightening for me to hear this, because I hadn't realized that I probably started scaring people back in 2000 when I was chairman of the retail arm of the British Music Industries Association with questions such as, "Are we comfortable with the fact that our industry is being eroded as we speak?" What I was trying to generate then, as now, I guess, was this idea of productive paranoia.

Productive paranoia is mainly referenced as a quality that is necessary in leadership or in anyone aspiring to be a leader. It is less of a requirement for those who are led, but the very best organizations, like Apple in its early days, are those whose leaders instill productive paranoia deeply within the fabric of an organization.

Individuals like Apple co-founder Steve Jobs understand that the fastest way to create success in a company is to fix a problem that the organization or the general market have. Fixing such issues, moreover, requires companies to never be comfortable or complacent, thinking that they have got the problem covered. That is corporate death, as far as Jobs was concerned. Where productive paranoia becomes something whose importance spreads from management to the shop floor, is when a distinct lack of it is in evidence. Quite frankly, as soon as a culture of comfort and complacency takes hold, anyone who goes along with it is not helping their company to grow. Chief executives come in for a great deal of criticism, but one of the qualities they mostly have in abundance is a focus on driving revenue, reducing costs, and solving problems. They have this focus because if they do not pay attention to these issues, somebody else will and they will be out. Consequently, managers who climb to become overall leaders tend to do so because they are productively paranoid.

Dyson's dilemma

A really practical example of someone who should have adopted more productive paranoia is Sir James Dyson. Hugely admired by business analysts and consultants, James Dyson is an illustration of someone who has created brilliant, market-changing innovations, and who is a good example of entrepreneurship. More recently, however, Dyson has lost the lead in the vacuum-cleaner market to a 100-year-old company called Euro-Pro. Euro-Pro has launched something called the Shark Rocket, and it has eaten into the vacuum cleaner industry that Dyson had previously monopolized.

How it did this in the US, and now increasingly across the rest of the world, was by benefiting from the lack of productive paranoia exhibited by Dyson. After its early years of disruptive, radical inventions, Dyson started to move more toward low-risk innovation, incrementally improving some appliances, such as hand dryers and cooling fans. Ultimately, what Dyson didn't do was continue to radically innovate in its core area of house-cleaning products. Dyson was comfortable in the knowledge it was the market leader. The company did not exhibit productive paranoia.

At the same time, Euro-Pro had been sitting around with hardly any market share for 100 years in the cleaning industry, until it decided to radically innovate with new styles and models of household appliances and committed to throw $130 million into advertising behind that.

You will remember the graph in chapter 3 which illustrates the reality of exponential change. True to that model, Dyson saw Euro-Pro as a low threat, and it is that perceived low-threat rating that Euro-Pro now used against Dyson. It was able to innovate, publicly and openly, while Dyson fell victim to the business poison of thinking ". . . but we're Dyson." What Dyson should have had was constant productive paranoia.

On the other hand, Procter & Gamble, the world's largest branding company, has put innovation at the heart of its company over the last three or four decades, not in terms of marketing or public relations but actually in terms of its investment. P&G's Brussels Innovation Centre is an outstanding example of what happens when a company is perpetually paranoid in a productive way. P&G has no belief at all that the products that generated the bulk of its profits in the last quarter are still going to be on sale in two years' time. The company does not believe that, because it knows that is how its market works. It has to constantly remind itself that what it is seen as producing now will eventually be useless, so it had better have something else to replace it with, because someone else out there is sure to be working on that very idea. Procter & Gamble has become the biggest family of brands in the world because of its productive paranoia. It is not something that it sees as revolutionary. P&G executives are traditional, seasoned, tie-and-jacket, comparatively straitlaced business people who completely understand that the next five years are not going to be anything remotely like the past half-decade.

How do you structure your business to have the same future-proofing as Procter & Gamble? The answer is that the first step is to align your purpose. The second is to enable the right people to be aligned with that purpose, and then have the willingness to continually change your view and what you think at any time is the right or wrong next step. Mix in a healthy dose of productive paranoia, which is essentially the certainty that if you're not creating something in response to the winds of change then someone else sure is. You can call this innovation, but the reality is that change is all that there is. The issue is whether you actually use that change to power your business in order to build it for the future, or try to block it out in order to make hay while the sun shines now.

My advice, in terms of generating a good sense of productive paranoia, is this:

1. Investigate what you're currently discounting as being a low, or non-existent threat, whether it's because you see something as potentially substandard, too futuristic, or any other shortcoming that you are imagining.

2. Identify what things would disrupt your business—not just in terms of competition but also in terms of changing contexts (for example, the landscape shift from bricks and mortar shops to e-commerce).

3. Integrate the above findings into your strategies moving forward, at the very least in terms of how things are constantly

monitored, but ideally in how innovation is directed and developed.

The advantage of productive paranoia is strategic, commercial, and competitive. It is the opposite of comfort and requires the willingness to continually repeat the three steps outlined here.

CHAPTER TEN

The Paradox of Exploitation versus Exploration

How do we go about getting people who are willing to change and possess productive paranoia in abundance to exploit existing business assets and opportunities, while also exploring innovations and new potential approaches? The answer is the concept of something I call "the paradox of exploitation versus exploration," which is the third element with which the Purpose blade needs to be constructed.

Many businesses are like an oil tanker. They move slowly and make the most of all the existing assets and resources that are already in place. Organizations have a requirement to make what they normally make, sell what they normally sell, but yet at the same time need to be thinking in a more agile and change-driven way. These companies need to simultaneously be exploring new ideas and territories in a faster way, just like launching a speedboat.

Paradoxes are different from problems. A problem has a solution or an answer, whereas a paradox can't be solved in a binary way, so therefore needs balance. If this tension between exploitation and exploration were a problem, then you could say something like, "Sink the oil tanker!" Yet what you might then end up

with is a potentially unprofitable speedboat with none of the experience and benefit that the oil tanker brings. Another answer could be, "Drown the speedboat!" but then you find yourself in a prime position just waiting to be disrupted by the perpetual winds of change, while comfortable on your comfortable tanker— which in reality is exactly the same as building a wall to resist change. Instead what we have here is a paradox that requires balance. We need to balance these two requirements, and find the most effective way to exploit what we already have and do, while exploring the new.

There are very few companies that have done this really well. One great example of a business that has created an amazing balance of exploitation and exploration is W. L. Gore and Associates. This Delaware company, best known for its invention of the Gore-Tex waterproof breathable fabric membrane used in all-weather clothing, is a sizeable organization, but somehow it balances the paradox so well that it launches frequent speedboats while the oil tanker chugs along. It uses little innovation teams that act fast, exploring new innovations and approaches. The teams achieve this by establishing a number of enabling structures. The first one is that information-sharing and peer-review are the norm. There's no hierarchical review; the main review is from your colleagues. Also, there's no protectionism of information, so everybody shares all information at once. There's no mention of, "Well you're not going to see what I'm working on because you'll take the credit for it," which I'm sure is an attitude we've all seen in many companies.

It's all about a strong focus on getting the environment right. The teams spend a lot of time in the best physical spaces that allow their staff to work together. They have team coaches rather than bosses.

These coaches are people who have experienced more. They are not chosen because they're more senior, or they earn more money; they've just experienced more about the particular problem they are trying to solve.

This organization has the belief that giving people the tools and the knowledge will bring out their best. Everyone is given the best tools to do the job. They trust people to do the right thing, and the culture creates the opportunity for everyone to make a meaningful contribution.

There's a high level of investment in team-building, and there's also a divide-and-multiply concept. As soon as the workforce on a project gets to over 50 people, it spins out; because there's no way when there are 20,000 people involved that the hierarchy is going to help that project grow, so they set it off on its own, just like a little speedboat. That spin-off operates on its own little system, but still linked in ways that support it to the main star. Gore's system limits bureaucracy in that way.

Within this firm, you're only a leader if people want to follow you. There's no appointment of leaders from anyone other than peers. The peers decide who leads, and the leaders only stay in charge if people still follow them. Along with this, there's a commitment to constant experimentation in order to test, learn, and improve. Gore sees its purpose as being to solve problems—it is one of the most productively paranoid companies I have ever come across. Given this purpose, the company's leadership is constantly looking for problems, and this is a collegiate focus. Rather than trying to work out who is going to get promoted, managers form teams around who is most passionate about solving a specific problem and who cares about it the most. The first version of Gore's Elixir guitar strings, for example, has now been iterated and improved more than a dozen times. The company never believes it has solved something for good; it is always seeking another problem that it can solve.

In this way, Gore is a great example of balancing the paradox of exploitation versus exploration. This is a proper windmill company.

However, if all of these things seem too far out of your reach currently, I have two pieces of advice that I would strongly encourage you to put into place as soon as humanly possible so that you can begin to balance this paradox yourself.

First, it is absolutely vital to have senior stakeholder buy-in, because if you're going to build a speedboat, you need to have a senior stakeholder in the oil tanker who can campaign for not sinking the speedboat. Otherwise, the speedboat always gets run over and sunk. This happens all the time when the people in charge of the oil tanker don't believe in, or buy into, the idea of the speedboat.

Second, you need financial redesign. You need to decouple the profit-and-loss sheet used for the oil tanker's business as usual, from the profit-and-loss sheet for the new, innovative approaches of the speedboat. If you don't unlink these sheets, the new business exploration looks too costly and expensive, and the existing business looks as if it's losing focus due to the investment in these new experiments. Remember, you can't actually do the financial redesign unless you have senior stakeholder buy-in. Ultimately then, these two pieces of advice are in strict order.

Refresh and review

To be able to flex your organization in a way that enables it to achieve real success in radically changing markets, your people, and particularly your leaders, need to be capable of adapting flexible mindsets. This needs to encompass being able to elevate the corporate purpose, innovate products and services, and develop the most efficient and productive processes to deliver the change that will be needed to survive. If nine out of ten businesses fail mainly due to the way that their people respond to events that destroy their companies, the decision-making capability of those leaders becomes absolutely key.

The crucial elements to this are the **skill and will** of your leaders and managers, the ability of the whole organization to be gripped by a constant **productive paranoia** that ensures it is always at the top of its game, and a way of balancing the paradox of being able to **exploit the current** opportunities while also investigating and **exploring new** and potentially disruptive ones.

Ask yourself:

Do your key leaders and managers have the ability or skill to adapt to change and the willingness to do so?

Do they accept that change is the only constant, and recognize that what made your business successful in the past not only will not guarantee future success but also could actively harm that likelihood?

Do you and they have a process that regularly tests the assumptions of the organization and its leadership?

Are you and they open to new ideas and thinking from both inside and outside your organization?

Do you have a strategy for tapping into the 98% of thoughts, ideas, and realities that we don't know that we don't know? The concept of productive paranoia addresses this quandary, for, without that, we believe that we know everything. Such a strategy could therefore begin with an acceptance that we do not know everything and progress to encouraging curiosity, seeking out new information, and changing company routines and realities.

Does your organization harness the power of productive paranoia? Are you constantly investigating what you're currently dismissing as being unthreatening, identifying what would disrupt your business, and integrating all of those findings into your future strategies?

How well are you getting people who are willing to change and possess productive paranoia to exploit existing business assets and opportunities, while also exploring potential new innovations and fresh approaches?

Are your people capable of transforming your business so that it can survive and thrive in a world of perpetual change? If they are not, what do you need to change?

Blade Three
PRODUCT

The blade of Product, which you could also call a blade of service, is whatever is produced, created, or delivered by your organization. It is perhaps best illustrated by the following story.

In 1847, a Hungarian doctor called Ignaz Semmelweis, who was working at a maternity hospital in Vienna, realized that the infant mortality rate of children with "childbed disease"—a condition that has since been renamed as cot-death syndrome—was far higher for babies born in hospital than for those who were born at home. This greatly puzzled him. The growth in the number of European hospitals in the early nineteenth century was a direct response to increases in the birth rate as an industrializing continent garnered and distributed the wealth and knowledge to sustain greater populations. By their very nature, hospitals were supposed to be safer and healthier places to have babies. However, Semmelweis came to this realization that the death rate was increasingly higher in maternity hospitals than it was for home births. When he investigated this apparent conundrum, he discovered that the reason behind it was that people tended to use soap and water for hygiene and cleanliness at home, whereas in hospitals, doctors were considered to be "gentlemen." Unlike

the failure of many of its outputs. When organizations concentrate their resources on well-designed, properly thought-through products, the profit invariably follows.

What the Semmelweis story illustrates is that throughout history, new inventions—in this case a more enlightened way of operating hospitals—create their own messes that need to then be fixed. Inventions begat inventions. People and companies fix something, and as part of that, they generate other problems that also need to be addressed. There is no finite point in invention; it is a cycle of betterment, and it's a falsehood to think that when we have fixed one problem we have not actually opened up new messes. Inventions require a choice between use and abuse. This innovation choice has existed since the dawn of disruptive human innovation, which arguably was fire on demand.

In my opinion, the domestication of fire was the first democratization of power. Until that point in history, the strongest physical bodies survived. Once fire was controllable, a weak person with the right flint and wood could take on numerous enemies. Fire was also useful in cooking, enabling us to digest foods that were problematic beforehand. However, fire could also be abused, and the result of abuse could well involve burning your own dwellings to the ground—or worse.

What happens with inventions is that individuals and organizations discover the uses of such innovations that are most productive for them. It flows from this that the invention on its own is therefore only as good as that use, which is at the heart of utilitarian theory. Mess-finding is a vital component of the product part of the Windmill Theory and the third element in the Product blade, as we will see shortly. But the point I want to make about Semmelweis's story is not about mess-finding. It is that product creation, development, and distribution is a dynamic, rather than singular, process. Whilst all of our blades are moving parts, because they need to be powered by the winds of change, inside the product component is a very strong requirement for mobility and evolution, which is driven by an awareness of what is happening and what biases are already in place. In Semmelweis's case, the prevailing cultural belief that gentlemen should not and could not have dirty hands meant that his innovation was not appreciated within that context, and 20 years of potential progress were lost.

Innovations, as well as existing business products and services, need continual refinement. However, the Purpose blade needs to be constantly linked to this process in order for these adjustments to produce sustainable value. Apple, for example, has built its reputation on design and innovation, but the company's idea of continual adjustment and refinement is to make more profits. If money-making is your main objective, your business is more likely to be disrupted by others because some of the most profitable ideas in the short term may not come from finding and fixing messes, but from spotting temporary price distortions or other inequalities, which certainly aren't the things that will enable a business to thrive into the future.

Once such temporary blips are resolved, the effectiveness of that particular profit-enhancing initiative peters out, the company switches its efforts to finding another such idea elsewhere in its organization or the wider marketplace, and the end result is a reputation for profiteering rather than reaping the rewards of pioneering a solution to a problem that benefits others too.

With all of that as the established context for designing and building this part of our windmill, let's start by looking at candles versus mirrors, the first section of the Process blade.

CHAPTER 11

Candles versus Mirrors

In the 1940s, Pulitzer Prize winner Edith Wharton said, "There are two ways of spreading light: to be the candle, or the mirror that reflects it."[56] What this means in terms of the way we view our product or service is the difference between creating something ourselves or allowing others to own the creation and then simply exemplifying and amplifying that. Airbnb, Uber, and Facebook all display mirror characteristics, for example. None of these companies are necessarily producing anything themselves; they are using the capabilities of others instead, and then reflecting those things back to their users and consumers.

Despite the overwhelming popularity of mirror-based business models today, that isn't to say you have to be a mirror to succeed in the modern landscape. When bringing a new product or service to market, you could also be a candle. In addition to that there are gradations and points along the spectrum between both of those, leading to what I view as hybrid models.

It should be stated from the outset that it is extremely rare to find a perfect, pure example of either a candle or a mirror in the world of business. The best way to view this is as a spectrum between the two extremes, with companies and organizations all fitting in somewhere on the scale.

These are the three primary business model options to choose from, and they all have various pros and cons attached to them.

1. The first one is a candle. That means that it sells or monetizes its own products or services directly as a retail or rental company, maintaining a direct relationship with the person who buys from it, the end user. A candle-based business is a "centralized" offering in the same way that a candle has its own flame, has its own wax, burns, and shines its own light.

For the sake of argument, we're going to call that candle Apple. It sells Apple products and services in an Apple store, to an Apple customer, who gets an Apple receipt, and who needs an Apple email address to operate an Apple iPhone or Apple iPad.

2. The second business model option is right at the other end of the spectrum, and is a mirror, selling or monetizing its products and services through a licensed third party, who can be viewed as an enablement framework to allow this. These are companies that could shine their own light, and could have their own wax, but they choose to enable other organizations, outlets, entrepreneurs, retailers. distribution functions, or their own franchise holders to be their light. In this arrangement, the creator of the product or service doesn't have a direct commercial customer relationship with the end user.

This model is characterized by an independent corner shop or general store, or a small online retailer that purely sells and distributes a variety of other people's products.

For the sake of argument here, however, we are going to call this model IKEA. Yes, IKEA is the name on the receipt for everything bought at an "IKEA" store, but as the company operates a franchise model (as do companies like McDonald's, Subway, and Gold's Gym), when you visit an IKEA outlet, you are not actually buying the product from IKEA itself. You are buying an IKEA product from someone who is an independent retailer who has bought a franchise of IKEA.

3. Finally, in the middle of Apple on one side being a candle, and IKEA on the other being a mirror, we can also see versions in between. An example of one of those would be a company that can sell directly, shining its own light, but that also enables other people to be the purveyors of their light.

    For the sake of argument again, we are going to call this one Amazon. Amazon can sell an Amazon product in an Amazon store to an Amazon customer—this is the candle part. It can equally be a mirror, reflecting someone else's light by allowing other traders to use its e-commerce platform to sell their own products using an Amazon check-out function. In addition to that, it can also be the web host for a competitor selling something, enabled by Amazon Web Services.

What is absolutely important to note here is that you have one of three relationships:

1. A direct commercial relationship selling your product or service to your customers, and therefore total quality control of delivery (candle).

2. At the other end of the spectrum, there is an indirect sales relationship with your customer. That also means a total assumptive guidance of quality control via your third party distributors (mirror).

3. And a middle ground, which is a hybrid, with some elements of the model requiring a direct relationship with the customer, and some having no end customer touch-point at all.

To be clear, the purest forms of these models are almost non-existent in business, as it is impossible to be 100% a mirror if you have even one instance of having a direct sales relationship with your customer. Equally, it is impossible to be 100% a candle if you have even one instance of a third party who sells your product to their customers. As I said before, it is a spectrum between these two extremes.

You might be thinking, "But hang on a minute, there are electronics stores that sell Apple products to their own customers, so how can Apple be a candle?" The reality is that Apple does not license its products to these other retailers. It sells its products directly to those stores, who then sell them on in turn to their customers. Apple is a pure candle that has both direct B2B and direct B2C relationships with its customers.

Equally, Uber, Airbnb, and Facebook do have a kind of direct relationship with their customers in that they own their data, and the transaction in some cases—but not the product or service. These companies are essentially enablement frameworks. They provide the ability and architecture for things to happen on and around them. Airbnb, for example, is in essence a website that enables someone who has something (a room) to be linked to somebody who does not have that commodity but who does have a need for it, albeit temporarily. The fact that these are frameworks or platforms means that it is common for there to be a closer relationship between a supplier of an on-demand service such as a taxi or a home and the customer enjoying renting them, than that of either party with the incumbent service platform (Uber or Airbnb in this case).

IKEA is a mirror because its primary sales operations are owned by franchise holders. Here within the Thought Expansion Network, we are also more of a mirror model than a candle, developing relationships with third-party suppliers like speaker agencies, bureaus, event management companies, and conference producers who then sell the professional speakers whose careers we manage on to their end client. Some internet aggregators of services also have the ability to be mirrors, if they are not directly selling the products they inform their viewers about to the end customer. Flights aggregator Skyscanner, for example, links travelers to transactional sites like Expedia and Opodo when they have chosen one of the options it provides information about. Other purer mirrors can be found outside commercial business, in organizations like Alcoholics Anonymous or Craigslist that have no centralized trading mechanism.

There are upsides and downsides for all of the models, and I want to go through each one so that as we're looking at our windmill blade of Product, we can decide how we can configure this component of candle versus mirror.

Just as users can control the quality of a candle's flame, one of the upsides of the first model is that you can control the revenue flow, due to your direct relationship with the end user. Another upside is that the relationship is something you can nurture and grow, remembering that in many cases the best customers are existing customers. One of the downsides, however, is that you have a limited market reach because it's just you; you're one candle. Whereas when you're a mirror, you can be reflecting as many candles as you like. The second downside is that you have relatively high marketing costs because you are actually the person who's funding every single thing that goes to market.

With the third-party mirror model—selling and monetizing indirectly—one of the upsides is increased market reach. By using affiliates, franchises, or similar, you can gain access to various markets that you wouldn't necessarily be able to get to on your own as a candle. Because of that, you also have lower marketing costs in theory. However, the first of the downsides is limited control of revenue because you can't always control the source of what it is you are selling, and you also cannot dictate the uses of funds when it's out in the market. Another disadvantage is that it is harder to evaluate how much the customers are actually attracted to what you provide. This is due to the fact that you do not have a direct relationship with the end consumer. A burger-buying customer at McDonald's is many stages away from the group's head office in Chicago, whose primary relationships are with its franchise-owners, who in turn control the relationships with their staff and consumers. A negative aspect of this is that it can be monumentally difficult for companies distributing their products and services through third-party franchises to control the quality of such offerings. IKEA has tackled this problem with IKEA Systems, an internal training mandate that serves as a highly detailed framework that franchisees have to adhere to. This framework exercises control by offering little scope for adjustment or interpretation.

Franchises operating under such tight reins might see these measures as draconian or dictatorial, but in IKEA's case its framework is the reason why customers can walk into stores under its brand name in any country, and receive an almost identical experience. McDonald's offers more control to franchise holders, baking in cultural sensitivity by allowing localization of menus to such an extent that the group's menus in Hong Kong are vastly different from those at its eateries in Las Vegas.

Scale is not necessary

To put it another way, when you are a mirror, the reliance on outsourced customer excellence is enormous—but you don't have to scale yourself in order to be successful. When you are a candle you can control the entire customer relationship, but the

165

only way you can scale is to take on another 40,000-square-foot retail unit yourself.

An interesting example of another type of pure mirror would be the Wikipedia online encyclopedia. It has no direct relationship with anyone, and it is therefore almost impossible to monetize this extraordinarily useful innovation in a sensible fashion. Organizations operating this sort of decentralized model, which is also used by Alcoholics Anonymous, for example, tend not to have a central product that they sell to people, so they cannot easily have a commercial model placed on top of it.

Over time, I have mapped out the suitability of various different industries for each business model. This is non-scientific and there are plenty of exceptions in my reasoning. However, for illustrative purposes, with regard to the first model of selling or monetizing directly, it turns out that it's quite suitable to most industries, slightly less so in technology, and slightly less again in fashion and beauty. These are industries where the requirement for the brand owner to be present is often less effective than having representatives or concessions.

When we look at the suitability of the mirror model, industries where there's a requirement for direct customer service tend to score lower. For example, the food and drink industries, and fitness industries score higher for the candle model and lower for the mirror model. If you actually have franchises, that's fine, but it's worth noting that franchise operator Gold's Gym may have quality-control issues if it can't always control the personal trainers in every single one of its gyms worldwide. They aren't always going to have the exact same level of standards. McDonald's also has an ongoing issue with the level of service, with significant systems in place to try to ensure every member of staff reaches a minimum standard of quality.

The upside, however, as I have alluded to above, is that this is a highly scalable approach and has low or no marketing costs. In terms of the downsides, there is very little or no control of the revenue because it depends on other people using the product or service, and you don't have a direct relationship with them at the point of sale. However, this often works well for the technology industry, which is why licensed technology platforms like software providers Salesforce or Google Apps, now rebranded as G Suite, make so much sense. In finance, the same thing applies. Take accountancy software start-up Xero, for example. We see the same model applied extensively within the entertainment industry, as license rights are where much of the revenue for the entertainment industry is generated.

When you are working out whether your business wants to be a candle, a mirror, or somewhere in between in order to make it more like a change-powered windmill, what you're really deciding is what type of relationship you want to have with your customers. Are you best off with a direct relationship with the end user, controlling the quality of your product, but more restricted when it comes to scaling your business? Or can you dispense with a direct end-customer relationship and therefore scale your enterprise more easily? Perhaps your product offering is best suited to you operating as a hybrid mixture of both. You can decide which one suits you more and whether the potential upsides outweigh the potential downsides. To give a little further guidance, if you're in a business where you've created something that other people could use that doesn't include a physical product, I would suggest the mirror models would suit best. However, if you are in a business that has a physical retail outlet that needs its own relationship with the customer, you may value the ability to sense and respond directly to your clients, despite the temptation to have indirect affiliates. Ultimately, if you can actually afford to lose the end-user relationship, but gain increased market reach, then you should move more toward the mirror-type models.

What you are really asking yourself here is whether your purpose in the first blade requires you to be a candle, mirror, or something in between. If your purpose is to create a human-level value through anything you provide to the market, in a way that is open to good influences and with an end user that you want a good, direct conversation with, it is unlikely you will choose to be a mirror. However, the anomaly is IKEA, whose entire purpose is "to create a better life at home for the many people." IKEA has calculated that it is more cost-effective to have a franchise model and pass the cost savings through to its customer base than to have a direct model with higher costs that would have to ultimately be met by its customers. IKEA therefore has a direct human purpose but operates a mirror system. It uses the profits of its franchise and self-assembly business models to reduce its prices for customers—one of the elements that enable it to be fully aligned with its elevated purpose.

The choice you are making here within your Product blade is based on your Purpose, and how your people then want to both manifest that Purpose, and choose the most apt Product suite in order to construct the third blade of the windmill powered by perpetual change. There is a range of options to achieve this, as we have explored. You can have a people-based Purpose that has a mirror-based outcome, or a non-altruistic, totally commercial, capitalist Purpose that your people manifest through a candle model with a direct customer-facing relationship, like a bank. However, if Semmelweis had started his voyage of discovery by deciding that he wanted to create a drug that he could sell in his hospital for a large profit, he would possibly have been less likely to have found something that has ultimately had a vast impact in saving people's lives.

CHAPTER 12

Transposition

One method of finding inspiration for products to launch that reflect a company's true, elevated purpose is to utilize transposition, the second section of our Product blade. Transposition is essentially about how we can come up with ideas by finding new expressions of methodologies that we can borrow from the external world and other companies or industries.

This is not to say that large, multinational companies do not have the necessary research, know-how, and expertise in-house that they need in order to be able to innovate. It is simply about acknowledging that inspiration is abundant in this world, particularly when we look outside of our own myopic tendencies that limit our internal universes to the definitions and practices that we already possess or pursue.

Transposition is a way of observing what is being done in another business model, industry model, or part of life or nature, and superimposing that onto your product or service offering that would perhaps provide an additional way of manifesting your purpose through your people.

If we look at Airbnb, for example, and assess its core methodology, it is clear that the company is essentially linking surplus to demand through accessibility, as we saw in chapter 5 when we were looking at the point of elevation in the Purpose blade. One person has a surplus in a space, another person has a demand for space, and Airbnb makes the link between the two people as accessible as possible. Now that we have defined their methodology, the most pertinent question is this: how can you take their methodology and use it to enable *your* purposeful main thing? How could you inherit or transpose Airbnb's model to your approach?

One can get a clue as to how this works by studying how such innovative companies move on to use transposition on themselves to further scope and scale their business. Why is Airbnb now getting into the food industry and thinking about how it can link surplus to demand through accessibility to tackle the problem of waste? It is doing this because there is a clear synergy there with its core, elevated purpose, but also because it is able to take best-practice methodologies of how some of the companies in the charity and waste sectors are going about meeting the needs of their stakeholders. Actually, Airbnb is free to apply its purpose to a huge range of potential issues, just as other entrepreneurs and companies can reflect on the subsector that Airbnb has helped create and consider how they could "Airbnb their business" by looking at what constitutes their own surplus that they could link to a demand in an accessible way.

If you look at any successful business around you, you can distill what its main thing is, in terms of what it creates, links together, or enables, and also the way in which it does that. Then the key is to transpose that successful methodology onto your own company's thinking and operations by imagining how it could link, create, or enable any functions that you already have, in a similar way. When I have said this onstage I have been astonished by how rapidly seeds of transposition thought take root in the minds of executives and entrepreneurs.

I remember addressing a Microsoft partner conference in Toronto and illustrating the point of transposition by referencing the Airbnb methodology as I have done here. I then asked what surplus the audience members had in their companies. One responded that they had an enormous surplus in bandwidth that his firm did not use. By transposing the Airbnb model onto their business, he saw that they could potentially allow that surplus bandwidth to be utilized by machines that can solve mathematical problems, starting a new income and profit stream at the flick of a switch. It's what Clay Shirky calls cognitive surplus,[57] when what you have too much of can be used by somebody else who needs it.

Companies in the Western world end up with many more resources than they actually need. There is surplus all around us. There are seats in restaurants and seats on buses that go spare. Unfortunately we tend to stick to the businesses that we are in, and know about, and we don't take the time to imagine that we can transpose or superimpose other business models onto what we do. The truth, however, is that there is more often than not a way that we could do this, and we even have new technologies like blockchain, which I outlined in chapter 4, that would enable these surpluses to be monetized by meeting demand in a really accessible way.

Imagine if all of the items in your house that you do not use could be written onto a "block," and that could then be linked to Amazon or eBay in real time. After, say, eight weeks, your computer could tell you which items of clothing you have not worn during that period, and evaluate the demand for those garments, taking into account interest, seasonal factors, and distribution. People wanting to buy the types of clothing identified could be notified instantaneously that those items exist or have spare capacity. With a simple click, you could sell or rent all of those items online. It may sound far-fetched but the technology to organize it is already in existence. And that capability of a real-time immutable source of visibility is something that our society has not, as yet, even scratched the surface of. Blockchain enables many other distributions of resources like this. It is a revolution that could be as big as the World Wide Web itself.

Opportunities for transposition can be as real for countries and governments as they are for companies and their executive teams. If we return to the example of Estonia, the country has developed itself as a digital society far advanced from much of the rest of the world to such an extent that it has been nicknamed e-Estonia. The nation that spawned technology innovations including Skype and the currency-exchange disruptor TransferWise, now a British-based business "unicorn," has succeeded with a methodology that is ultimately about linking governance to efficiency through capability. The governance in Estonia's case is of a country, while its efficiency makes it easier for people to enter and leave, list companies, get married, get divorced, or buy a house. This is all enabled through technological capability.

How could you take Estonia's methodology and enable *your* purposeful main thing by applying it? How could you inherit, or transpose, Estonia's model to your approach? Governance could be the way we govern how our product is made, how it is sold, or how the price is set. How could you make things like that more efficient through using technological capability?

We can see transposition opportunities everywhere. Let's look at the example of crowdfunding platform Kickstarter for a moment. All Kickstarter is doing is linking belief to production through investment. How could you link what people believe in to production through investment? This is transposition, and you can apply it to anything you observe, provided you can assess the core methodology and then ask yourself, "How can I enable my purposeful main thing by transposing their methodology to my approach?"

Think of the growth opportunities for fast-food companies if they embraced health criteria in their menus. The main chains have gone partly down this path by giving healthier options alongside full information on the calorie, carbohydrate, protein, and hydrogenated fat content of their signature dishes. Yet imagine the additional success that could come if McDonald's, Burger King, and KFC transposed the successful methodologies that the dieting industry has successfully applied to monetize healthy recipes into millions of pounds. But such moves cannot merely be marketing gimmicks. They must be properly thought out, scoped, and executed. It is not about having a salad wrap on the menu, or painting the furniture green. The application of transposition could be a way of turning fast-food giants into genuine health companies, which in turn would address all sorts of regulatory issues that otherwise may one day threaten their very existence.

Transposition can therefore start as a defensive strategy. Look at the criticism that IKEA used to receive for the ecological impact of its products and the way it has now ploughed millions of pounds into an environmental agenda that can stand comparison with most companies in the world.

Returning to the example of McDonald's, the burgers company clearly knows that the world is moving toward a more quantified capability, with people understanding more about what is entering their bodies and bloodstreams, and being expected to take direct responsibility for their health. Very soon, people will eat a Big Mac and know precisely how it will be digested, and affect the body's cholesterol and salt make-up. At the moment, it is deflecting such worries by simply reiterating that customers can choose the salad options in its branches. It has to protect its profits, which are in the burgers. Longer-term, however, that company and others have to think about where they go in this era of perpetual change. Transposition of some of the dieting industry's proven methodologies would be a good place to start.

Transposition can involve uncomfortable challenges like these that would necessitate major disruption. When I was chairman of the British Music Industries Association's retail committee, I proposed unsuccessfully that we could look at piracy in the music industry as a business model that we could adopt legally. Even though I didn't know it at the time, I had hit upon the idea of transposing a methodology that existed elsewhere, and using it to further our own purpose-driven agenda. I wanted to look at what piracy was really all about, which was linking content to fans through the Internet. That's all that piracy was doing, and I suggested that we should apply that to the music industry in full. Content in our context, I suggested, could be a band's guitars or sheet music: underutilized assets that could be monetized for the benefit of the owners. My idea did not meet with a welcome reception, however. Indeed, the feeling on that committee was instead that someone should sue the chief executive of the Internet for enabling piracy to rob creative people of the fruits of their under-rewarded talents. Believe it or not, a consultant was employed to find a person who was the nearest there could be to the Internet's CEO, and a cease-and-desist letter was faxed to the identified person, who turned out to be the head of an advertising agency in France! My idea of transposing piracy onto the music industry was absolutely ridiculed. It actually brought back the feeling of being bullied back in the playground when I was a child. I was very roughly moved into a side room at one of the committee meetings and told that this was the last time that I would use the words "Internet" and "music" in the same sentence. I later wrote a little book entitled *The Survival Guide for the 21st-Century Retailer*. I never sold a copy, and even when I gave it away to people in the music industry, everybody there professed not to have read it. However, all that I forecast became personified as iTunes and Spotify—perfect examples of what we could have created had we utilized the transposition that I had tried to suggest.

Transposition is hard. In the music-piracy example, for instance, if you simply distill the "main things" within that concept to being content, fans, and the Internet, you could indeed argue that the methodology could be applied to any other business. My suggestion therefore was that we should create a legalized version of piracy. However, "piracy" at that stage, and possibly still today, was an incredibly emotive term that was being seen as something that was destroying livelihoods. It was extremely difficult to divorce the negative connotations of the term from the very attractive business opportunities that it did indeed present.

That brings us onto the subject of messes, and I will just address the mess that was the music industry at the time as a link to the next chapter, which is about "mess-finding," the third section of the Product blade. At the time all of the above was going on, nobody in the music industry knew much about where to find the sites, such as Napster, MP3.com, and Kazaa, that facilitated illegal music-sharing. So the awareness issue was the first mess, which I believed could be addressed with public announcements and signposts about how to download music legally. Second, there was a tremendous trust issue. These sites were illegal with no obvious chief executives or boards of directors. Even the people who used file-sharing sites did not all trust them. And the third mess was the security issue, with millions of viruses unleashed on computers and networks through the illegally downloaded files.

I wanted to counter these three messes with a proposition that would have been tremendously secure, transparent, accountable, and accessible. But the answer was an emphatic "No." What happened next to the profits of the new recording industry is now a matter for the history books.

Mine is just one of many missed opportunities. Think how easy it would have been for any of the world's taxi systems to have launched something like Uber, or for a hotel chain to have launched a spare-room system equivalent to Airbnb. People tend to stick to what they know, and change can be the enemy of the competent, with leaders preferring to maximize what they have already identified for short-term gain. But next time you dream about your new venture, be sure to involve transposition in your thinking.

CHAPTER 13

Mess-Finding

When you've decided whether you're a candle or a mirror, or a bit of both, and you have perhaps identified some business models and methodologies that can be transposed onto your business, another way of empowering the Product blade for your full windmill is by finding a big fat mess to fix.

As I see it, where there is a mess, there is a market.

If we look back in history to inventions such as the steam engine, automated vehicles, and the vending machine, they were born of necessity to such an extent that it is now a cliché to say that "necessity is the mother of all invention." However, my version of this for the current age is that *where there is a mess, there is a market*. Early versions of the three inventions above, and more, were actually created by Heron of Alexandria, a mathematician and engineer who lived in Egypt in the first century AD, because engines and dispensers were what were most needed at the time. Heron's purpose was to fix problems, and he was well ahead of his time in the solutions he devised.

The advent of maternity hospitals made the increased birth rate manageable in nineteenth-century Europe by providing a dedicated resource where people could give birth, but as we have seen, the germs spread in these facilities actually ended up killing more babies. Pasteur discovered the ultimate solution, but the unheralded Semmelweis had specified the initial problem.

It may be that there are few things left that humanity can invent that are as useful as the wheel, for example. Yet that is probably a fallacy, with opportunities limited only by our imagination. In the meantime, it is easy and fun too to find messes that need fixing and envisage how these could be things that your business commits to solve.

If your company is in video streaming, for example, have you thought about the unmet demand from people who fall asleep in the middle of watching something and would like their show to be paused? Netflix has done just that with its "smart socks" that sense when wearers doze off and automatically pause the movie. Could this be elevated to people who find it hard to fall asleep? Napflix, another innovation akin to Netflix, has created "The Walking Chicken," a one-hour animation of a chicken walking around a Minecraft game. It has been streamed more than 100 million times. Understandably, it helps people doze off.

I often used to wonder why washing machines didn't also dry, fold, and iron your clothes. For years, I moaned about this onstage, and eventually a company called FoldiMate launched to do just this. It was a mess just waiting to be solved. I also used to be frustrated by walking on Lego bricks that my son left all over the house. I mentioned it to Lego, and the Danish company created Lego Slippers, which protect feet from the extraordinary pain that standing on a piece of Lego causes.

Elsewhere, a company called Megasus has created the world's first running shoes for horses, fitted with no nails or iron. Another company that has created "selfie shoes" allows people to take pictures of themselves by popping their phone in a slot in the toe of their shoe, and then getting the perfect angle for a photo by raising up their leg! There are now also bike tires that can't get flat as they are made from polymer blends that offer durability, whilst remaining cushioning and resilient. Another company is working on drones that light up the paths of people walking home in the dark along unlit streets, in order to address safety issues. Along the same lines of thinking, there is now a glow-in-the-dark bicycle path in Poland that is charged renewably by sunlight. Then there is Skunklock, a bicycle lock that, when tampered with by a potential thief, emits an odor that makes them immediately vomit.

In social media, a NiceBot has been developed to say pleasant things, balancing the ugliness of online trolls. IKEA, meanwhile, has redesigned its entire furniture range, as I referenced earlier, to make it snap together so it can be assembled without tools in a maximum of 30 minutes. Lego has made a bike helmet that resembles the hair of its famous plastic figures, to encourage children to wear one. The product is now one of the world's bestselling bicycle helmets. Virgin is planning a supersonic plane that can cross the Atlantic in 200 minutes. A company called The Breakup Shop pledges to help people do exactly that, eliminating the mess of ending a relationship. A Chinese firm is making headrests in the shape of people's laps and torsos, so that those living alone can feel some semblance of human comfort as they sleep.

Other messes that have been fixed recently include Amazon's Fresh Pick Up venture, which is using last-mile logistics to enable Fresh Pick Up, a service permitting people to pick up goods a short time after ordering them online. Graphene filters are enabling seawater to be transformed into drinking water, potentially eradicating a shortage of drinking water in the right places, which is truly one of the world's biggest risks and messes.

These great examples are the exceptions, however.

What messes are there that we still need to fix? When you figure this out, you are on the path to enabling the survival of your company in a world of perpetual change. Where there is a mess, there's a market. And where there's a market, there is an opportunity for your business to innovate for everyone's benefit.

One can either address a demand that may not yet exist but is easy to envisage as being created soon, or alternatively focus on an issue that resonates strongly enough to have a clear probability of fueling demand. The hardest part of bringing anything to market is getting other people to want it. Innovators and inventors may find their great idea extremely intriguing, but if the market doesn't agree, it will just end up being another wacky invention that didn't work, or a solution that remains in desperate search of a problem. Solving real-world messy problems goes a long way toward validating market demand before we embark on the design and creation of a new product or service.

There would be strong demand, for example, for an actual fix to catching viruses, given that humanity already knows by and large how, when, and where they are transmitted, and what could perhaps be done to stop them. Or in other areas for solutions to email phishing frauds or drink-driving. Why does a car ignition not link to a breathalyzer so people cannot physically start a car without their alcohol level being under the legal driving limit?

All these innovations are already, I believe, technically possible. So is the reason that they have not been fixed a matter of will or purpose? Or is the maintenance of some of those messes actually providing some attractive short-term gain for some vested interest or party?

The emphasis on mess is to reduce the risk of low or slow demand. You may remember Sir Clive Sinclair's C5 electric vehicles. One of the few people to do so, my father actually bought one for us when I was growing up—an amazing piece of technology with a 10-minute battery life that nobody had any real use for. The better way of thinking up new business ideas is to find the latent, existing demand. Drive-thru takeaway restaurants in the USA actually date from the era of cowboys on horseback. The cowboys didn't want to get off their horses, or have anywhere convenient to tether them while they stopped to eat, so the local merchants created a way of serving them in the saddle.

Fixes to messes have driven the invention of some of our favorite products, but there is a difference between messes that we know exist and those that we were not previously aware of as messes. We also don't necessarily have to be the first person to bring a solution to a mess to market. When Steve Jobs unveiled the iPhone as a device that could hold people's entire music libraries at the same time as it enabled them to communicate by phone and also use the Internet, consumers at once saw the logic. The iPhone was actually launched nine years after the first such device, while camera phones were pioneered in Japan, apps had been around for years, and Internet access had been popularized by BlackBerry. So the mess that Jobs announced he was fixing was not new. But it had never been addressed before in such a beautiful way.

Similarly, Tesla was not the first American electric car company. Now it is the second-largest car manufacturer in the world in terms of book value. So it is perfectly possible to address a mess that has already been addressed by somebody else. Google was not the first search engine. Other companies were doing that, the best-known of which was perhaps Yahoo! But Yahoo! was only indexing a portion of the internet, while Google's Larry Page and Sergey Brin had the vision of indexing the entire World Wide Web.

Could other unmet needs be remedied? Car-emissions pollution is a major unfixed problem. So is the number of people with some medical conditions where a better cure would probably be available if attention was brought to focus on the problem by making available some serious, organized crowdsourced funding.

If a small fraction of the families of people with, say, Alzheimer's Disease each contributed £100, that could create the largest research fund in the world for a single condition. And a bonus pot to incentivize the researchers and scientists to come up with viable solutions could end up making some of them billionaires while also solving a major medical issue.

It is of course more appealing to imagine solutions to messes that nobody seems to have thought of yet. One innovation that perhaps no one ever asked anyone to make was allowing tickets for theater and music concerts to be bought online. But try telling your teenage children that if you wanted to go to a show in the past you had to call up the theater, or send a check in the mail with a self-stamped addressed envelope, which you hoped would arrive before anyone else had bought the last ticket! It's an example of a mess few people had articulated, but it would certainly be regarded as a major mess now if online ticketing did not exist.

Some fixes to messes relate to clear themes and trends, such as Internet-enabled disintermediation, which also led to solutions including online stock trading and flight and hotel booking. However, this mess-fixing also produced an array of new messes, such as music piracy. And there are many other messes originating elsewhere that have never been fixed.

As an example, let's take the situation where you have to touch the door handle to leave the bathroom after you've washed your hands. That's a massive mess. It's a mess because a lot of people who haven't washed their hands proceed to touch that handle, which negates the benefit for you and anyone else who has indeed cleaned their hands, which promptly get covered in germs again from the handle.

On a similar theme, hospitals and some other workplaces offer antibacterial gel stations for people to sanitize their hands on entering their premises, but the process is entirely voluntary and at risk of being unmonitored. If such organizations really want people to use that gel, would they not be better off placing the dispenser outside automatic sliding doors that only open when triggered by the gel being released from the pump into the visitor's hands? This form of choice architecture is an example of mess-finding. Hospitals can prevent people from bringing germs onto their premises by realizing that using antibacterial gel is not yet an intrinsic part of people's behavior, and then changing designs so they have to use gel as part of the contract to opening a door or perhaps ordering a coffee. Only then will they find that the true mess will be properly solved.

Another mess could be the large number of people who chew on the end of their pen—and having found the mess, fixing it could mean manufacturing a pen with teeth-cleaning substances inside it.

Pillows that are streaked with eye make-up in the morning could be seen as a mess—and one that could potentially be fixed if manufacturers made a pillowcase that also contained eye make-up removal properties.

Why cannot bars be redesigned so it is easier to queue at them, or for bar staff to know who is next in line to be served? Missed delivery slots are irritating, particularly when the only evidence that someone attempted to deliver your package is the tick-box card dropped through the letterbox.

I fully appreciate that some of these examples may seem a little ridiculous or trivial, but the largest innovations with the biggest market opportunities often share one crucial element, regardless of how silly they may seem—they fix a mess. Some messes may seem like superficial subjects, but they're not at all insignificant when their solution creates a multi-million-dollar business opportunity.

If enough people are looking for a solution to even a seemingly irrelevant mess, then there may well be a viable opportunity to be found.

KFC in India realized that a lot of people feel panicky while they're eating their deep-fried chicken because their phone is running out of battery. Because they want to enhance the experience of eating their chicken, they designed and trialed an integrated phone-charging port into the serving box, so that customers could charge their phones while they ate.

In London, lonely women are paying fifty pounds an hour to be professionally cuddled by strangers.

Then there's something called the Pilot Earpiece, coming out next year, which goes in your ear like an earplug and can translate any language being spoken into your own language in real time.

Some major messes are all too apparent. Most people find the limited battery life in today's smartphones to be an irritation and annoyance, making those periods when we are without power, communication, and networks unconnected and unproductive. One day, somebody will invent a device that only needs to be charged once a month and can do the same or more as any other mobile phone, and work on any operating system that customers want. Even if this phone is dropped from a heady height, it will not break. The screen will never crack, and the phone will be as slim and convenient as anything that is on sale today and will cost one-tenth of the price. The market will shift enormously toward this new product, the way it did when the first iPhone was introduced and incumbents like Nokia were left in its wake. Ironically, Nokia phones had much better battery life than modern smartphones, but the rest of the Finnish company's proposition quickly eroded because it was not fixing the other problems that smartphones solved. The reality is that batteries with the power we need to keep our cellphones charged for weeks already exist. What does not yet exist is a pricing mechanism that can make such batteries affordable on mobile-phone contracts.

The more you look around, the more messes you will see that need to be fixed. A major danger to ocean life is the plastic six-pack rings from beer cans. To address and fix this deadly mess, there are now edible rings that are digestible by marine life instead of deadly if they find their way into our seas.

Elsewhere, inventors at Google have considered one of the most lethal elements of a pedestrian being hit by a car: the person bouncing off the car and being flung into a wall or onto the asphalt. So why not create a sticky car that can stop a body from being flung off the car, and therefore reduce the potential crash injuries? Mess fixed.

Then there's a company in the UK that has produced a wristband that, when you spend too much, delivers a 255-volt shock. What's truly amazing about this is that the band is also linked to the smart thermostat in your house, so that if you're overspending, it will turn down your heating as well—resulting in you ending up shockingly cold. On the subject of electricity, it is impressive that all kinds of gadgetry and apps now enable householders to switch their home heating on and off, or up and down, from the comfort of their offices. While they are away from their home, they can also use sensors to alert them to distress signals such as dogs barking or glass being broken at their property. Meanwhile, governments are mandating power companies to develop smart meters that can encourage consumers to use less energy, reducing carbon emissions and mitigating some of the enormous mess of climate change. But why is no company linking these two pieces of technology so that people can see the results of their temperature changes in pounds and pence or dollars and cents?

Equally, as you look around, there are lots of messes in terms of sitting on planes for very long journeys. Some companies have experimented with a novel approach of firing the plane super-fast out of the atmosphere, so that it goes up high enough, waits for the world to turn around, and then goes down to its intended destination, which is now below. It's quicker than traveling in a linear way. Mess fixed (hopefully!).

Going through an airport with kids can be a total nightmare, unless they could sit on the back of some sort of fun transport system. And when you're traveling with a pet, the water that you're trying to give it to drink in a bowl tends to slosh around and spill. So why not invent one that has been designed to fix this very literal mess, and doesn't spill? When there's a group of you at home who want to get takeout but can't agree on which particular style of food you all feel like, how about a service that enables you to order from multiple different restaurants at once, but delivers everything together? Before you are tempted to discount these inventions as trivial or irrelevant, bear in mind that Trunki, Road Refresher, and Hungry House are all £100-million-plus companies now because they created solutions to those specific problems.

If we're testing products on animals for the cosmetics industry, why not print out 3D skin that can be used instead, so there is no further need to use animals for these tests? If you wear glasses and that's a great big hassle of a mess for you, then why not go for the surgery that gives you eight times superhuman vision?

For someone who wanted to disrupt Uber, why not fix the mess within what Uber calls "surge pricing" that charges a passenger more at peak times? It is said that Uber even know when your phone battery is running out, and they can increase the price according to your level of urgency to confirm your ride. One start-up has looked at this, seen the mess, and is attracting new customers and taking market share with their promise to pay you back your Uber surge prices as credit to book your cab rides with their company. Mess found, mess fixed.

Uber, by the way, is constantly on the lookout for new messes it could fix. They have seen the multi-takeout services like Hungry

House and Go Eat and figured out that they have large networks of drivers, and could do food delivery in a much better way. So now Uber are trying to widen their market and scale their offering by fixing that particular mess.

Another mess in today's world is that we're surrounded by huge amounts of information with little time to focus on mindfulness. This is the mess that apps like Headspace and Calm are addressing: the fact that we're bombarded by an increasing volume of noise in our lives, and we could be happier and healthier if we gave ourselves some headspace.

If you're still wondering how you can go about all of this, here is a four-point toolkit of how to spot, and address, mess. It's called the Mess Management Matrix.

1. Start with the most obvious mess.

You probably already know in your industry what the most obvious messes are. You know what needs to be fixed. In every market, the companies inside it absolutely know what the messes are themselves. Globally, it may well be that the lack of enough drinking water in the places of most human need is one of the biggest messes we are confronted by. However, going down a level to your specific area of expertise, there are absolutely other messes there that everyone will understand. Ask yourself what obvious messes there are in your industry. If we are honest with ourselves about the parts of our market that are broken, then we might just be inspired to do something about fixing them. Are there things coming down the line that we know of that are going to create obvious messes? What are we going to do about those?

2. Don't create more mess.

Often when a mess is fixed, those solutions themselves can create additional messes that then also need to be addressed.

Yes, of course, if a Chinese factory can replace 90% of human workers by robots, increase the production by 250%, and subsequently the defects drop by 80%, then it would seem that the mess of human involvement has been solved! Unless, of course, while we're busy implementing that scenario, we're also creating a world that actually wouldn't have humans in it. The thing is, we often have mess-fixing situations that can look fun and friendly on the outside, until the much bigger consequences and messes are revealed. We have to think very carefully about that, and if any additional mess is created by our solution to the initial problem, then we must have some ideas about remedying that too.

3. **Modify existing technologies to suit the mess in the most relevant way.**
   How can we use the things we've already got to suit the mess in the most perfect way? For a company that creates drones, they might find it fascinating to think about the technical capability of their product, and the continued betterment they are pursuing. If we match that to the fact that a huge amount of pain and suffering in the world exists in places that we can't easily get the necessary relief to, then why don't they create a drone that's biodegradable, perhaps, which could fly into those hard-to-reach places, drop medicine or aid, and then disintegrate?

   How can we think about using the standard technology that we've got and that is already in place, and flip it in order to fix a mess? The high crime rate in India, for example, is in part due to the fact that a huge proportion of wrongdoing goes undetected because there aren't enough police. However, there are a lot of people walking around with camera phones. So when you enable the camera-phone people, armed with "weapons of mass communication" to be reporters, using the micro-journalism devices in their hands, then the crime rate goes down.

We know the problems exist, so how can we use our existing resources and technologies to fix them?

4. Keep the mess solution remarkably simple.

Even when the idea that fixes a mess has a huge degree of complexity behind it, the trick is to simplify the presented solution. We have all, I'm sure, been somewhat guilty in the past of making things so complicated for people that they just don't understand what we are trying to do. You can always tell when a B2C company gets it wrong in this way, when they say something like, "Hey, why don't you buy this 'BRAND-43PZ73H'!" There's no one outside the company who understands or even cares what that means, which is a huge barrier to anyone buying into the solution you are presenting.

When people go into a DIY store, they're not going in to buy a drill—they're going in to buy the quarter-inch hole. We want the solution. We don't want the thing in between. We need to be mindful of constantly closing the gap between what people have and what people need.

It is crucially important, in terms of our Product blade, that we integrate mess-finding and fixing into our innovation and development strategies. This section is just as vital as our Candle versus Mirror choice and how we transpose the methodologies of others to uncover new areas of potential. When you adapt your mindset to view the world around us through a mess-finding lens, you will see that opportunity is everywhere.

Refresh and review

Ultimately, *where there is a mess, there is a market.*

When we combine our blades of Purpose and People with our blade of Product, we can find enormous potential markets as we link our elevated "main thing" to a mess that needs to be fixed. This is where the greatest opportunities reside. We can also find inspiration when we look at other companies and distill their business model down to its core elements. When this is then transposed onto what we could produce and create, or how we could operate, then we can adopt existing best practice from the market, and utilize it ourselves.

What does your organization produce or serve up for its customers? Have you become so focused just on the profits that you are losing sight of when some of your company's outputs become less optimal? Are you putting earnings before products, or concentrating your resources on well-designed, properly thought-out creations in a way that the profit will invariably follow? Remember that while inventions and innovations in products and services need to fix previous messes, they can also create new ones to solve that provide business opportunities for you or others.

Ask yourself:

*Is your business a candle that creates light directly or a **mirror** that reflects the light of other candles?*

What type of relationship do you want to have with your customers? If you want to have a direct relationship, that's fantastic, but you cannot scale in the way that you can with a mirror—or "decentralized"—model. If you don't care so much about the direct relationship and you trust that other people will provide a good enough level of quality control for your product, then you can achieve scale.

*Are you able to utilize the creative power of **transposition** to find new ideas by understanding the distilled methodology that* *you can borrow from the external world and other companies and markets?*

What do you see being done and admire in other industries that you could apply to your own?

Do your competitors have something that your organization lacks and can develop an effective response to?

Is there an unmet need in the market that you can fulfill by changing the definitions and practices of how you operate and see the world?

Is there a big fat mess that your business could fix?

Try making a list of ten messes in the world, or your specific industry, that irritate you and that you would like to see fixed. Then consider whether there is any way that the main purpose of your organization could be elevated to fix that mess. How can your company use this opportunity to make itself indispensable for the period of the need that it is fulfilling?

For all of this to work, of course, we then need to ensure that we have the best process in place, otherwise nothing will actually happen. We need processes to link our purpose to our people, and for those two elements to link to the product (or service) that we produce.

Blade Four
PROCESS

The Process blade is unusual among the four in that it runs across and interacts with all the others. In fact, none of the other blades work properly without a set of processes. The Windmill Theory would simply fall apart without the enabling processes to make everything work together.

Your business can have a clearly defined, elevated, and well-specified purpose that resonates with you and the world. It can also have an impressive range of leadership executives and other people who are completely aligned with that purpose and are the very best in their roles. You can also add to that the very best products and services that solve messes and meet previously unmet needs. If you lack the right processes to execute on all this promise, however, then it is highly unlikely that you will fully equip your business with the agility and adaptability that it needs, not just to survive but to truly succeed in a landscape of constant change.

Alternatively, an organization may have some of the most leading processes in the world, but if there is not a rigorous, clear, well-understood, and resonant purpose along with the right people involved who have the skill and will to manifest that purpose into the products and services that are its outputs, then world-class processes are essentially all it has, and little, if anything, will be produced that is capable of being bought, sold, or possessing value.

With all the other elements properly in place, the Process blade is then a critical element without which nothing is possible in business. Without it, the end result will only be negative, or at best suboptimal, no matter how much inspiration and toil goes into it. This is the "how" of business: the tactics that enable the organization's strategy to fulfill its objectives and ambitions. The process is the critical enabling structure that drives all movement for our windmill.

Process is also the blade that is the least well understood and appreciated. Most people I explain the Windmill Theory to end up being pretty comfortable with the logic behind the first three blades of Purpose, People, and Product, even if they do not then go and implement them in their businesses. It is the Process blade that is generally disliked and deprioritized across the board by senior directors.

Interestingly, chief executives hate the Process blade for completely different reasons from why most shop-floor workers don't like the sound of it. Line employees associate process with pedantry, administration, systems, rules, and supervisors. Executives, however, know that it will involve re-engineering the way their whole business runs—and in actual fact it will do that much, much more than they can even imagine. Integrating the Process blade in your company will require a reorganization of so many things, from how you bring ideas into the company from the external world, how you democratize the talent pool, and perhaps how you collaborate with the general public. Just for starters. Consequently, the Process blade is the one that most businesses find it hardest to install in their companies.

Practically, however, the Process blade governs everything. Nothing works properly or well without some kind of process behind it. So it is reasonable to suggest that if you are looking to build an adaptive, agile business that will stand a better chance than most of thriving and surviving in the years ahead because it is going to flex and mold itself around the changes coming down the track, then you had better instill some kind of order or procedural working into that organization. If you do not, it will have no chance of performing effectively, and may even damage your company before the changes that you have not prepared for properly finish you off.

I believe that everything in business falls into one of three categories: input, production, and output. Input covers everything that comes into a company, and it can include people, information, inspiration, trends, competitive behavior, news reports, and social disasters. Production means anything that is created as a product, service, manifesto, purpose, or public relations statement. And output includes everything that leaves an organization so as to go somewhere else. That can be the information produced in the organization that's given to members of staff when they go home. It can also take the form of output into the market as a new product, or as a press release to the media, financial statement, or communication materials for analysts. Input and output can be received and transmitted internally as well as externally. Production is the active part between those two categories.

Within this triumvirate are three components of what I would define as making up process. These form the three sections of our Process blade: frameworks, filtration, and coordination. Frameworks are effectively the rules that govern an organization's processes, while filtration concerns the level of filters applied to everything that happens within production for extreme efficiency and success. The third is the coordination and integration of every single thing that happens, and it establishes the links to every other part of the windmill. I will look at these three blade components of frameworks, filtration, and coordination in the following chapters.

When everything is in place and works together effectively, then the windmill can operate, impacting every area of our business. Take product innovation. The process for product innovation needs to be a porous, dotted-line mechanism that takes in information from the external world, runs projects in sprint cycles on the inside, and operates teams on a cycle of testing, learning, and making constant improvements. It also needs investment into projects that potentially have the chance of failing, but the mindset is one of continual learning, enabling decisions to be made regardless of whether the short-term outcome met original expectations.

Or consider what will happen when machines are able to undertake half of all the jobs that are currently carried out by humans. Actually, that's a conservative yardstick, and it will probably arrive a long time before you expect it to. But do you have a plan for that? What is the process behind that plan? What new technologies will you embrace; which will you reject? And how will you know before you do either which ones are most likely to succeed? To answer any of those questions, you need to have processes in place to manage your research function, the flow of information both externally and internally, and the way that those things are then translated into tangible action points.

What will our society do if 50% of all factory workers become unemployed? Ultimately, a company's purpose and people need to be put into place in a strong and clearly defined way so that the decision about what happens to these workers is already pre-constructed by your purpose. With all due respect to some of the companies that are beginning to automate, this is not what is generally happening.

Foxconn Technology Group, the Taiwanese company that assembles computers, phones, and computer games for businesses ranging from Apple to Sony and Nintendo, has already discarded tens of thousands of workers, replacing them with robots to carry out their job, as I've previously mentioned. Foxconn's effective purpose is efficiency of production. Its view of people is that it wants to eliminate as many of them as possible. Its products will grow far cheaper to manufacture, thereby offering even more profits for their business partners. And their processes will increasingly be based purely on automation. The result will be higher levels of unemployment, which in turn will require greater natural and governmental resources. Viewed in terms of macroeconomics and sociopolitical problems, the actions of contractors like Foxconn promise to have a devastating effect on the world, perhaps in spite of their operating model.

On paper, I believe that Foxconn's business model is pretty sustainable, since it is tackling a manufacturing reality that humans are not necessarily the best machines for repetitive tasks. Regardless of how this plays out, I stand firm in trying to help those who believe that the doomsday scenario is not inevitable and are willing to undertake the work that is required.

This is where the Process blade properly kicks in, because this is the part of the windmill that really gets things done. It is relatively painful because it calls for you to look at any processes that you already have in your organization, to question them, and then to insert different enabling structures. But it is this blade that is the key to making the whole windmill work effectively to harness the winds of change, and it is what makes organizations and individuals adaptive and flexible so that they can respond to change effectively.

Netflix is one company that demonstrates that some processes can be automated, and workers displaced, without the net effect being negative. As we know, Netflix was a physical renter of physical DVDs, when they saw that increased connectivity and bandwidth would allow households and individuals to watch films over the Internet. These changes meant that they had to close the warehouses where workers would sort, package, and mail DVDs, but it also led to Netflix opening a film-production unit as the battle for viewers turned channels into production houses. Netflix now employs production managers and script-writers rather than envelope-stuffers, and interestingly its overall headcount has gone up. The company meanwhile is now the same size as Hollywood in terms of movie distribution.

This sort of fundamental change evidently requires willing-ness among staff who can be up-skilled and learn new abilities to perform different roles as they engage with the changing nature of their company. The Process blade is therefore especially closely linked to skill and will, the first section that we examined in the People blade.

So with these ideas and examples in mind, let's look at Process frameworks.

CHAPTER 14

Frameworks

For our fully functioning windmill to operate efficiently, there need to be established frameworks inside it. Frameworks can be used for any element of business, whether it is how information gets in from the outside, or how innovative new ideas are generated. Whatever the requirement may be, there are three absolutely vital primary characteristics of an effective framework. It needs to have:

- Porosity. A framework should be porous and penetrable by design, to enable information and data to flow in and out of it. Frameworks should have dotted lines, not hard ones, around them. They need to be permeable to influences and ideas from the world around them. And they need to be able to breathe out into the external atmosphere too, inhaling and exhaling like a living, functioning being.

- Pace. Many frameworks in companies are not built with speed in mind, but constructed with other priorities such as compliance or risk management. Whilst these are valid concerns, they sometimes come at the expense of things happening fast enough to keep up with the speed of change. The pace at which a framework operates needs to be in harmony with the rate of change in the outside world, and the speed at which the aspirations within your company are developing. I have seen in my career many organizations with 18-month development timeframes that every week hold meetings taking around three hours, followed by a review process every six weeks. Sometimes, in the review process, the development timeline gets added to, which is why one company might launch something after three years of planning and development, while a competitor outflanks it by doing so in just three months.

- Responsiveness. Porous frameworks that have the ability to work at pace are not effective if an organization is not able to respond to inputs that are arriving both internally and from the ever-changing external world. Responsiveness governs how the processes within a company trigger behavior, actions, and new thinking so that it can better fulfill its objectives and purpose.

One of the best cautionary tales about process is Zappos.com, which until 2015 was consistently ranked as one of the world's most favored companies to work for. Set up in 1999, when its founder Nick Swinmurn was wandering around San Francisco looking to buy a pair of shoes and could not find any with his exact specifications, the company grew swiftly as an online footwear retailer and also expanded to offer clothing, accessories, homeware, beauty items, and other products. Zappos.com, named after a shortening of *zapatos*, the Spanish word for shoes, also developed a true passion for customer service, with a focus on wowing its consumers. Zappos chief executive Tony Hsieh is on record as saying that when the company asked itself what it wanted to be known for, his answer was that he didn't want it just to be about shoes. He didn't even personally like shoes. He wanted the firm to be known worldwide not for what it sold but for how it sold it. Zappos was to become a byword for exemplary customer service. Now there's an elevated purpose!

After a pivotal moment involving a shopper who wrote to the company to praise it for the customer-friendly way in which it had responded to her experience of ordering two pairs of shoes that were both unavailable, Zappos realized that this was one of its main points of difference. This focus also rubbed off on the company's internal culture, in a great illustration of what it looks like when a company's purpose is properly integrated. The firm polled all its employees on what they thought should make up its core values and ended up with a list of 37 culture ideals and 10 core values, which were put at the heart of how Zappos acted in all activities from hiring to firing. Zappos was soon seen in corporate and consulting management circles as a key example of how an inspirational purpose could find, incentivize, and retain the best talent. On top of all of that, the products, as well as the service, continued to delight consumers. Amazon eventually bought Zappos after being impressed with the demand for its products and the high price-to-quality ratio. People inside and outside Zappos believed in the company's purpose of changing the way that apparel was sold and its four Cs values of clothing, culture, customer service, and community, with customers seeing the company's high-quality products as a brilliant manifestation of these stated priorities. Everything was going swimmingly. Then Hsieh bought an entire corporate process called Holacracy with the aim of organizing the company's administration in a better way.

Designed to empower everybody within a company, Holacracy is a platform of self-organization that claims to be able to help companies structure and scale their operations for growth. Hsieh was an enthusiastic convert. "Research shows that every time the size of a city doubles, innovation or productivity per resident increases by 15%," he said in 2014.[58] "But when companies get bigger, innovation or productivity per employee generally goes down. So we're trying to figure out how to structure Zappos more like a city and less like a bureaucratic corporation."

The theory sounded appealing. Zappos would switch from a traditional hierarchical corporate structure to Holacracy's model, with employees acting more like entrepreneurs, self-directing their work instead of a reporting to managers who told them what to do. The new platform was seen as an ideal way to remove roadblocks and encourage innovation to come from anywhere within the company. What on earth could go wrong? Well, quite a bit, actually.

The Horrors of Holacracy
Developed by a company called HolacracyOne, Holacracy stands for holistic democracy. Established by Brian Robertson, who used the process to experiment with more democratic forms of organizational governance at Ternary Software, a computing company in Pennsylvania, its core process is a specific social technology in which authority and decision-making are distributed throughout self-organizing teams, rather than being vested in a management hierarchy. Robertson developed Holacracy in 2007 when he was a 35-year-old computer programmer, having taught himself coding at the age of six. He believes that Holacracy is a far more efficient way of running a business, as in his view most organizational problems are created by humans. The process sells for between US$50,000 and $500,000, depending on customer size, and the sale includes the visit to the buyer by a process engineer who redesigns every facet of corporate process in terms of input, production, and output.

HolacracyOne convinced Zappos of the need to strip apart its entire corporate processes and replace them with their systems. The result was an utter disaster, with one-third of staff leaving Zappos in 2015, losing the company its place in the best companies to work for lists for the first time in its history. Rather than continuing to be known for its extraordinary customer service and the core values that it had previously exemplified, Zappos quickly became renowned for being run by a system that simply did not work.

The episode has become a case study of Zappos as a company, of the Silicon Valley environment, and of Holacracy itself. Technology writer and venture capitalist Om Malik has accused Silicon Valley of having an "empathy vacuum."[59] At least one book has been written about why Holacracy doesn't work. Holacracy has been accused of empowering processes, rather than people. In its clamor to attempt to eliminate human emotion in the name of efficiency, it is seen by critics as imposing layers of bureaucracy and adding levels of unnecessary psychological stress to workers, who are given strict rules as to how to behave in meetings, with small talk banned and employees having to obey prescribed instructions on the types of things they are allowed to say. Staff are not encouraged to have opinions in this system, and there has been a backlash from employees at many companies where their processes have been introduced. The teams in these companies have been protesting against a rigid, formulaic approach, and stressing that they are real, human people, not computer programs, so they need to be listened to and treated accordingly.

After trying out Holacracy, Julia Culen, an executive coach and management consultant, wrote a post entitled "Holacracy: Not Safe Enough to Try."[60] She wrote, "I felt like being part of a code, operating an algorithm that is optimized for machines, but not for humans. The circles I was being part of did not feel empowering at all but [were] taking away my natural authenticity as well as my feeling of aliveness. It was fully unnatural and we were disturbed by rigorous protocols and procedures."

I am personally astonished and even appalled that Holacracy has been adopted as a central organizing process by thousands of companies across the world. This is a process that is not porous. It does not allow companies to operate at pace and it is certainly not responsive. In fact, it is insular and protectionist. Even according to Robertson himself, it can take at least five years to work. It is also designed so that it does not respond to any external stimulus, because it is based purely on battening down a company's hatches and forcing it to stick to its knitting. It is everything that the Process blade of the windmill that allows organizations to power themselves through change is not. It is seen as a bad thing within companies operating these systems for staff, customers, or internal or external commentators to have opinions. In fact, there is no such thing as a view, opinion, or judgment within a process like this. Data alone is king. Nothing else matters. Employees who vent an opinion out of turn in a meeting at a company where this is being implemented are "black-marked" and lose points. Porosity is seen as something negative and is to be avoided, as that would allow the system to be infected with unregulated input. Teams are replaced by "circles." Members are only allowed to speak to other staff in a circle once a week and are not allowed to raise their feelings at any time, speaking only about data. Points are given for how workers spend their time, and these are taken into consideration when renewing contracts and releasing staff. Challenges can only be raised via a function called "tension processing," which lays down highly restrictive procedures for how they are expressed and then resolved.

Based on everything I have read, studied, and personally observed regarding this process, I believe that Holacracy has sadly caused some companies to have some serious commercial problems. At Medium, the blogging platform founded by former Twitter executive Evan Williams, Holacracy was deployed across the firm. Medium had brought in $150 million of investment, but Holacracy's model determined that the return on that investment through the company's commercialization department had not produced any data, and therefore those people should be sacked. So Medium's entire commercialization team was fired. Next, it told the company to ignore the trend that is seeing media content worldwide become increasingly free of charge. Not being porous to outside influences, the process insisted on a different set approach. The result is that Williams has taken his company off the system, saying that it is the wrong kind of process, is getting in the way of the style in which the company wants to operate, and is preventing it from being open to new ideas. "We need to create an entirely new business model and approach," he said when announcing this change.[61] But damage has already been done, with staff fleeing, investments eroded, and the company's reputation suffering a major hit.

There are many other examples of where this has absolutely not worked for companies (although for those organizations managing to successfully utilize the system, then I can only say I am glad that these exceptions exist, and applaud your success). It is the embodiment of what happens when you remove all of Blade Two from our windmill. Williams wanted Medium to democratize information and enable people with a story to tell it on a wide platform with deep reach. That's an admirable purpose, but the process through which he has carried it out has completely disregarded the people part. The blogging platform is a great, slick product, and it is plainly well intentioned, but the complete lack of a porous, pacey, and responsive process has left the company in tatters. Removing two of the four blades of a windmill does not leave much of a windmill, and certainly not one that can benefit from and be powered by the winds of change.

Holacracy itself is unabashed, declaring a healthy number of customers and an undaunted confidence in the system. And because it can take at least five years to work itself out, it may take time for everyone to realize what a terrible idea it is. This particular company is not the only attempt to create an algorithm-led process system that can manage companies in the age of Big Data. In Silicon Valley, in particular, the mindset of many of the firms there makes this idea highly attractive. But in my experience and strong opinion, it is a misguided and highly damaging concept that does nothing to make companies agile and capable of surviving change, and instead creates unhappy workplaces and makes organizations highly vulnerable to talent loss and more.

Fortunately, Holacracy, and the few other platforms closely modeled upon it, are the only real examples of a widely adopted process framework that is utterly awful and simply does not equip organizations with the flexible mindsets they need if they are to harness the winds of perpetual change. All I can hope is that more people begin to see them for what they are, and instead adopt and implement change-powered processes that help to drive their future success.

Let's be clear. Process-management tools can be helpful to businesses, and there are some genuinely effective ones, such as AgileScrum, Kanban, and Waterfall. But those that are most successful have a dependency on what *you* put in: your reasons for using them, your data inputs, people involved, and general business context. It all depends on what is put into the process tool or methodology. In a sense, it does not really matter what the tools are. Getting value from the framework depends entirely on the inputs. When things go wrong with process frameworks, it is because companies seek an advantage by building in a methodology that is more primary, or seen as more important to itself, than the outcome it is supposed to be driving.

Process frameworks need to be highly porous to allow information about what works and what does not work to flow from and through both the inside and the outside worlds. Companies need to be open to hearing what the cleaning staff, receptionists, interns, secretaries, cashiers, and others have to say about their processes and how they affect the employees that are bound by them. Some of the best ideas for companies to improve themselves come from the shop floor, as workers tend to know better than most other people, and usually far better than the senior executives, whether a given process is working. Internal collaboration, cooperation, and communication are vital, as well as an organization's awareness of what people outside its walls are saying too.

Procter & Gamble's Connect + Develop framework is the polar opposite of Holacracy's systems. It is a porous framework on which any collaborators from outside the company are able to work together with P&G employees on projects within the group's walls. Unilever's Foundry platform is also very heavily inspired by a collaborative ethos. Nobody knows as much as everyone, and porous frameworks utilize this power by letting in opinion, expertise, and other people's views about what is, and should be, going on.

It's all about being porous, having pace, and encouraging responsiveness. However, in laundry products, for example, one of the reasons why Unilever has not been able to make significant inroads into Procter & Gamble's 38% of the global market is that the Anglo-Dutch company has lagged far behind the American group's openness to ideas from the external world. Almost 50% of P&G's new products now originate from crowdsourced innovation through its Connect + Develop program, but it is only comparatively recently that Unilever has launched its Foundry initiative, with the aim of achieving the same results. It has taken a decade of P&G's success through crowdsourcing to convince its closest competitor to try a similar process.

The other factors of pace and responsiveness also matter as much as porosity does. One problem that highly porous frameworks can face is that the amount of information coming into them can slow their processes down, and mean that they are no longer able to work at pace. And even if a porous framework does act with pace, it may not be designed in a way that empowers an organization to respond well to lessons and learnings.

Nokia's response to Apple's launch of the iPhone, for example, could well have been challenged from a framework perspective. From my observation, the group's problem in responding seemed like a processing issue, and not necessarily one of understanding, or lack thereof. I'm sure that Nokia had plenty of external input from qualitative and quantitative researchers, as well as a virtual army of trial groups and test markets, but its lack of speed and responsiveness was obvious. A lot of people inside Nokia may have said, "Well, that's just the way we've always done things," or, "We're successful enough not to be disrupted," or quoted any of the other business poisons. But the company's poor level of responsiveness to what turned out to be a fundamental threat to its existence played a key part in the Finnish company losing ground and ultimately the competitive battle so quickly.

Process frameworks need to be that combination of porosity, pace, and responsiveness, so that the machine in your company defined by the triumvirate of input, production, and output can ensure that it has a validity that is contextually relevant in the business environment of the day. It is then able to bring to market products that customers want to buy, or launch services that people want to use, in a way that suits the modern expectations of consumers or corporate customers in a business-to-business landscape, and uses technologies that are also relevant and understood in the marketplace. The operating essence of your company also needs process frameworks that are synchronized with the requirements of retail channels and resonate with staff.

Process frameworks are not all about dealing with information. Their input mechanisms allow anything that can be input externally or internally to enter too. Similarly, their production mechanisms do not just produce physical products. And their output mechanisms do not exclusively output things that go to market. This process mechanism is the way that a windmill can turn in the wind. These inputs and outputs are the ultimate enabling forces. Traditional business theory does not teach us that ideas from the outside world can be super-powered into internal ideas that a company can then exploit. Neither does it hold that business plans need to be altered much more than every three years. However, my personal belief is that current business-school thinking is fundamentally not valid in a world undergoing an increasing pace of change. Perpetual motion requires everything to be on a continual review process, with an accelerant component inside it so that the rates of input, production, and output increase over a set period without compromising on quality or commoditizing products or services.

Now, here's an example of a marketing framework that I designed for one of the largest companies in the world:

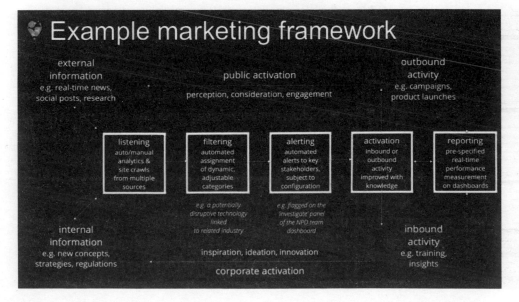

This is an example of a porous, rapid, and responsive framework, used in the context of a marketing function. Remember, frameworks should be used for every operational element of your business, and this is just one example. As you can see, there is a direct link between externally and internally generated information that is then activated in the public domain, or internally. The resulting activity that happens outside or inside is then fed back into the start, and the framework continues to respond, evolve, and revolve.

W. L. Gore's process systems are a great and positive case study too. The company operates a range of frameworks that enable slick input, production, and output mechanisms. It has extreme clarity of purpose, based around the passion for endless innovation that led its founder, Bill Gore, to leave chemicals group DuPont in 1958 to start a business that could imagine new uses for polytetrafluoroethylene (try saying that quickly!). That passion led to the discovery of Gore-Tex, as well as the launch of Elixir guitar strings and also Glide dental floss. Gore's employees are free to talk to everyone at the company any time they choose, which is just one facet of its strong culture emphasizing fast decision-making, collaboration, diverse perspectives, and a long-term outlook.

The company's purpose is the simple yet all-encompassing notion of "life betterment." Its core values are freedom, fairness, commitment, and consultation with associates before it takes actions that it might consider to be under the group's "waterline" and therefore able to cause serious damage. And it has a fabulous set of processes that are porous, pacey, and responsive.

Gore believes in a flat management structure, with the company arranged as a lattice, connecting every individual in the organization to each other. There are no management layers between the chief executive and the employees. Its teams are self-managed, there are no organizational charts, and job titles are resisted. The company asks every member of staff plus their families and friends to identify a mess and bring it to them. It then assesses the pace required to suit the level of experimentation that each project might require, and looks at which parts of the organization are best suited to solving that particular mess. Category enthusiasts tell the associates in the company what they are working on, and whoever finds it of interest and can bring relevant skills to the table then joins the team. That is the entire management decision.

Gore also allows people who are not on its product development team to make calls on which products need to be pulled from development. One manager at the company was famed for handing out trophies to associates who used the clarity of being relatively external observers to kill off unpromising projects. Employees are encouraged to write up what they learned from the exercise and how the company could have made the decision to kill the project sooner. The result is high staff retention and a sustainable, highly profitable company whose work is evident around us from synthetic blood vessels to the retractable roof at the Wimbledon tennis complex in London.

Now that we understand the critical requirement for our process frameworks to be porous, pacey and responsive, it is important to state that this can lead to quality control often becoming a key issue. This therefore calls for a function that filters the good from the bad and keeps organizations on the right track. That function is called filtration, and it is the next section of the Process blade.

CHAPTER 15

Filtration

When companies have porous process frameworks, how can they sort through and manage what enters from inside and outside, which will allow the right products to be created; their people to be happy, loyal, and productive; and their elevated purpose to be achieved?

The second section of the Process blade addresses how we turn information into understanding. There's a vast amount of information in the world, and it is increasingly hard to understand what matters. There is so much material to consider that we need to go through a process of working out how to identify the most valuable information and then turn it into understanding that we can act upon.

This is what I call "filtration". If organizations lack a filtration process or mechanism, they can end up being bogged down in random, unwanted data, ideas, and communication that is not relevant to how they operate. Companies need to be open or porous to new ideas, but they also need to monitor what's happening, reach an understanding of what it means and why it matters, and then create an execution plan. The starting point for filtration is to be very clear about what it is that you are actually trying to do, not just in terms of your purpose but also with reference to your product pipeline, go-to-market strategy, and sensitivity of supply-chain dynamics. Without understanding what you are trying to achieve, you cannot effectively filter out the elements that are getting in the way.

The best companies have effective filtration processes to police this issue. Procter & Gamble's Connect + Develop platform is crystal-clear about what it is that the company is trying to achieve, what it is looking for from members of the public, and how and when that information will be used. Starbucks, meanwhile, uses a filtration methodology in My Starbucks Idea, the company's collaborative movement that generates suggestions for improving the business. Again, very detailed instructions are given as to how this system works. Employees submit ideas, management decides upon a shortlist, staff then pick winners, and teams look at how they harmonize with other initiatives before applying and executing on the selected ideas. In Unilever's Foundry, similarly, the company makes it clear what sort of people it is looking for and exactly what those people will be expected to achieve.

The first part of filtration is therefore about clarity of objectives, and then absolute transparency about the expression of those objectives so that the relevant people inside and outside an organization understand what it is that you are trying to do, as well as how you are planning to achieve it. You therefore need to have a framework for this filtration process.

An example of a company that does this exceptionally well is Tesla. It has a brilliant set of frameworks in place, including ones for filtration. In the spirit of being porous, rapid, and responsive, Tesla has given away its patent rights for anyone to use. The company has opened up its entire research and development function in this way. It made this announcement, stating, "Yesterday, there was a wall of Tesla patents in the lobby of our Palo Alto headquarters. That's no longer the case. They have been removed, in the spirit of the open source movement, for the advancement of electric vehicle technology."[62]

Tesla has opened itself up to outsiders in this way because it does not believe it can create the entire infrastructure that the world needs for electric vehicles on its own. It needs other companies to invest and innovate too, so it therefore allows the flow of some information out of the company. Entrepreneurs can go to application programming interface (API) repositories such as Github and obtain Tesla-based code to develop new car innovations. The company's promise is that it will not sue anyone who uses its code in this way.

When others then build on Tesla's ideas, the data management that comes from the cars that are built using that technology feeds back into Tesla's mainframe, so that it can learn from the data generated by the cars, and improve its own products. Information is shared in this way without the threat of legal action. Tesla can compete with others, but equally the others can compete with Tesla, but using Tesla's technology. This is an example of a porous, responsive company that has a huge amount of pace. The process becomes the product, the product becomes the service, the service becomes the innovation, and then the innovation shapes the company itself. Such an empowering filtration process is therefore at the crux of the Process blade.

The Asian city-state of Singapore has created something called One Service, so that any service provider, whether inside transportation or whether in groceries, construction, or the fitness industry, for example, can list itself using a Singapore API, given from the government, free of charge. The public is given free access to the One Service, so that anyone can click through and see all the service providers that have integrated their API inside their systems. The idea is that people in Singapore can purchase whatever they need at a single checkout, because everything is linked together. In this way, Singapore has created a porous, pacey, and responsive framework for an entire country.

Google has done something similar with the API of Google Mail, Google Maps, and even the company's core Google search engine. Many of the services that compete with Google's search engine are actually using Google's API to do so. Amazon Web Services, meanwhile, has enabled almost all retailers operating online to use AWS's cloud-based service to actually compete against Amazon. This is an example of the kind of "business judo" that I learned in order to protect myself against being bullied at school, and it is what some of the world's best companies are using now to increase their competitive ability. If Amazon's competitor wins by selling a product to a customer, then Amazon still wins too: it has played a part in the venture, with the competitor paying to host its sales platform on AWS, and it has gained valuable data from it about what works. And if Amazon's competitor loses the sale to Amazon, then Amazon, by definition, has still won. Companies acting like this, therefore, keep winning, but their collaborative filter means that this happens in a way that moves the market forward. Amazon's purpose, remember, is to allow consumers to access and purchase anything. Google's is to organize the world's information and make it universally accessible and useful. And Tesla's purpose is to preserve humanity through sustainability initiatives. The processes they are using here are bang in line with these motivations. Their objectives are very clear, and they are communicated lucidly so that people understand how and why to use them. This is one part of filtration, which involves setting out a company's stall.

Apple, by the way, takes an opposite approach. It believes it is creating products and services that people don't yet know that they are going to want, so the company does not need to bother taking anyone alongside it. If there are products and services that emerge at the end of this process, they believe that they will be adopted widely just because they will be best in class. The company's track record over the past two decades is indeed hard to argue with in this regard, but continued corporate agility to respond to perpetual change is about ensuring that organizations can survive and thrive over much longer timeframes. So it remains to be seen whether Apple can achieve that on a 50-year view, as Gore and others have done. I would also ask even the most fervent Apple fan to identify what messes Apple is actually fixing right now. In terms of its processes, opening some of its windows, even fleetingly for one day, and allowing other inventors to send in ideas of how Apple could grow might produce some interesting results. If Apple is not going to be porous to other people's ideas, then every bet it makes over the next 10 or even 20 years has to be right on the money. And we all know that past successes do not guarantee future ones—in fact the opposite is often true, due to the false comfort factor that success can bring.

Companies do not necessarily have to ask people for a consensus on what they want. I am also not suggesting that porous frameworks need to allow every piece of feedback or useful potential product information to come in. Instead, it is that porosity, coupled with a great filtration process, that allows companies to find business models that they can transpose and messes that they can fix. Porosity also does not mean that organizations should knock down all their doors and windows. It means that there is a latch on the window, rather than the brick wall secured with lock and key that a lot of company processes have in place.

My preferred way of constructing filtration mechanisms is to build them in the same way as most machines: input, production, and output. This means that the first question regarding what goes into a filtration framework is, "What information is the most useful and valuable?"

To address this, I recommend something I call the Attention Management Matrix, which is simple enough to populate and

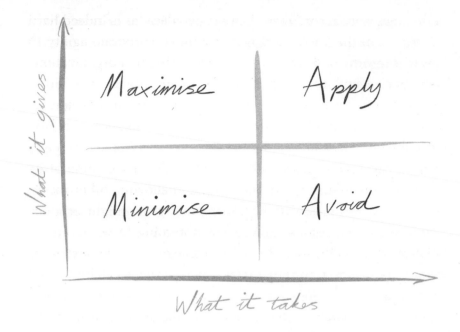

extraordinarily effective to apply, but actually very hard to find in use in most corporations today. The Attention Management Matrix is essentially a process of looking at whatever you are faced with from the input side of your machinery and seeing where best to apply management time and effort when you can assess the benefit that the associated effort creates.

The matrix is constructed on two axes. One plots how accelerating each idea will benefit you in terms of adding value, energy, and momentum to your team's products and designs. The other axis measures what this will cost in terms of cash, energy, and time resources. When you plot these onto the graph, your eye should be drawn to the items that require only a low amount of resources for a high rate of return. These are things that you should absolutely be maximizing. The ideas that require substantial resources but do also carry a high return should have effort applied to them, as they are still creating worthwhile results. In contrast, the notions that do not take a lot of effort but also don't give many benefits in return can be given low priority and minimized, while the activities that would cost a lot for comparatively meager returns on investment must be avoided altogether: they are unnecessary and worthless uses of your time and resources.

Over time, the more effort we apply to some rewarding ideas, the fewer resources they should take in time and energy, moving into the category of those things we can be maximizing. So the matrix can be amended and adjusted over time. Conversely, it never ceases to amaze me how much effort we, as individuals and companies, put meaningful amounts of time into in return for virtually no tangible gain. Think about how much time you personally spend on Facebook, for example, in return for little more than some transient social capital. Or how much money companies like Zappos are spending on expensive off-the-shelf process methodologies like Holacracy, where it takes at least five years to spot any efficiencies gained, may deliver no return at all, and might even cripple the business.

I would recommend the Attention Management Matrix as an input audition framework for any company, or individual, in order to understand what's important and requires applied focus, and what simply does not matter. It is a highly practical and pragmatic way of filtering everything and everyone that might come into your life or organization and ask to be allocated some of your resources.

In addition to that particular tool, while we are talking about distinguishing signal from noise in order to be able to make wise and profitable strategic decisions, another way to understand that is to look at the following steps, and ensure that all of those elements have been considered, designed, and put into practice.

- Be absolutely clear about your overall objectives, understanding precisely what it is that you are trying to achieve and why.

- Implement a filtration framework that enables what is happening both inside your company and externally to power in a very fast and responsive way all your other frameworks, including what you produce, provide, sell, and how you market that and liaise with customers.

- Decide which ideas to feed into your operations, by evaluating which ones will yield the most resources in proportion to the cost and effort they take to operate.

At this point in this account of change, it is valuable to look at whether such process frameworks should stand on their own or whether they are better linked to the Purpose, People, and Product blades of the windmill. That's the subject of the third and final section of the Product blade, which is all about how the blades can be integrated, consolidated, and coordinated.

CHAPTER 16

Coordination

The third section of this Process blade looks at how it works with all the other blades and sections to fulfill the purpose of this whole exercise and make organizations fundamentally more sustainable: able to survive, thrive, and succeed in times of perpetual and extreme change that will otherwise harm and destroy them.

It is critical for the entire windmill to work as a single unit. The windmill comprises these four component blades, and all of them are absolutely integrated with one another. Every single element of the structure needs to be integrated with every other element, and there is an overall process for achieving this.

For example, the way that you should view the development of your people—which is a process in its own right—needs to adopt the three key elements that an effective framework requires. So a process to develop the people and talent of our second windmill blade would:

- Allow their feelings to harmonize with yours—a porosity point;

- Happen at a fast pace so they feel appreciated;

- Be responsive to their ideas and thinking in alignment with their overall objectives and the overall purpose of the firm.

In this way, you can apply the logic of the Process blade to the way that people are hired—and it can equally be applied to the way your products are sold into the marketplace. You can also employ the process logic for how you develop and elevate your purpose in the first place, because one of the key requirements of an organizational purpose is that it should always be in context and relevant to modern times. If the purpose you are serving has absolutely no validity in this day and age, it is very unlikely that the environment around you would allow you to manifest that purpose in a positive or successful business outcome.

Your definition of purpose therefore needs to be porous enough to allow itself to be perfused and influenced by your understanding of the mood, tone, opportunities, and risks of the external world, and inside your own company too. It also needs to be created at a fast enough pace so that you don't procrastinate and spend time immersed in corporate navel-gazing when you need to be running the business. Then it needs to be responsive enough to how the organization feels.

For instance, the first section of the first blade is elevation. Let's imagine that you have already established your higher-level vision or mission, and you have worked out the methods of specifying clearly what that purpose means for your people. For them to take action by testing, learning, and improving, they require frameworks that are porous, rapid, and responsive.

Or ask yourself how you could enable your staff to be in a more harmonious environment by using a mess-finding process to deduce how your employees operate. In thinking this way, you are taking the third section of the Product blade and applying it to the whole of the People blade.

If you have a process of customer relationship management (CRM) that is porous, fast-paced, and responsive in how you deal with your existing customers, could you transpose this CRM process so that it could be used for new product development? In thinking like this, you are taking the second section of the Product blade and applying it to the beginning part of your supply-chain process.

To take yet another part of the windmill, let's look at the idea of candle versus mirror. Your choice of business model is based on turning information into understanding through whatever knowledge framework you have in place. Without one, you cannot decide whether your business model would benefit from being more candle-like or mirror-like. Whether your business has existed for years or is in the process of being set up, you have a choice of the model that best serves your future chances of success. The candle–mirror spectrum illustrates your options when it comes to distribution, which affects how you relate to customers and grow as a business. It is never too late to think about this.

There are many variants of this coordination and interoperability. Each blade and section can be applied to each other blade and section, and there are no limits to how many times this can be done. In fact, I suggest that you test every part of each blade on every other blade—and that you do this as an individual person, in addition to the perspective as a key executive in your company or organization.

Your organization, remember, operates a triad of a machine in terms of inputs, production, and outputs. And on a personal level, you have a trio of perspectives in terms of interpersonal, intrapersonal, and extrapersonal perspectives, covering everything that happens inside and outside of you, and between you and other people. Test your own level of skill and will, and your own individual level of porosity to the outside world. It's a useful, and revealing, starting point.

The reality is that the Windmill Theory is not just a theory, it's a practice. It is what allows us to design our businesses for perpetual success, because we have enabled them to be powered by change.

Every blade, section, and methodology that you have read about over the preceding chapters is fully applicable to every other. The Purpose blade is applicable to the Product blade, which is applicable to the People, which is applicable to the Process, which is applicable to the Product, which is applicable to the Purpose. It just keeps on going.

The ultimate effectiveness of the windmill comes when absolutely all the constituent parts are fully coordinated and integrated. But always remember what defines the ultimate, highest-level purpose of this windmill in the first place.

It exists so that, as the winds of change are blowing, you have designed and built a structure that continually powers your business for success in a world of perpetual change.

Refresh and review

Process runs across and interacts with the three other blades of Purpose, People, and Product. Without Process, none of the other blades work properly. While Process is the blade that is least well understood and appreciated of the four blades, it is pivotal to the success of the whole windmill that is being powered by perpetual change. It is also the hardest of the four blades to install into a company.

Ask yourself:

Can you reorganize and dynamize how you bring ideas into the company from the external world, democratize your company's talent pool, and collaborate with the changing desires of consumers?

Can you identify what in your business falls into one of the three categories of *input*, *production*, and *output*?

Within these three functions, do you have effective processes for **framing** what it is that you do and how you do it, **filtering** what you allow in and out of the organization, and **coordinating** and integrating every single thing that happens and its link to every other part of the windmill?

Is your process for product innovation a **porous**, dotted-line mechanism that takes in information from the external and internal world, runs projects in sprint cycles on the inside, and operates teams on a cycle of testing, learning, and making constant improvements?

Are you able to make investment into projects that potentially have the chance of failing, but that enable a mindset of continual learning, enabling decisions to be made regardless of whether the short-term outcome met original expectations?

Have you considered what will happen when machines are able to undertake half of all the jobs that are currently carried out by humans in your business? Do you have a plan for that likelihood and eventuality and do you know the process behind that plan?

Can your process frameworks operate at pace? Is adaptability and speed of response a critical factor in their development? Can they change rapidly if the rate of change in the outside world requires them to do so?

Can your company's process **frameworks** respond to events that happen both internally and externally? Can the processes within your company trigger behavior, actions, and new thinking so that it can better fulfill its objectives and purpose?

Are your processes porous like W. L. Gore's or inflexible and impenetrable by the external world, like the practices of Holacracy?

Is your company able to **filter** the information and other inputs coming into the organization so that they foster better understanding of what matters to the business, rather than tie the business up in useless clutter?

Are you absolutely clear about your overall objectives?

Do you understand precisely what it is that you are trying to achieve and why?

Is there a system of frameworks that enable what is happening both inside your company and externally to power in a very fast and responsive way all your other frameworks, including what you produce, provide, and sell, and how you market that and liaise with customers?

Are your processes harmonized properly and effectively with the three other blades of Purpose, People, and Product?

CONCLUSION
Build for Success

"When the winds of change are blowing, some build a wall, and others build a windmill."

I have often wondered about the origin of the proverb that started this book. Personally I think this is probably one of the oldest sayings on record that relates directly to how we have an option in the way we choose to handle change.

As is now hopefully apparent if you've made it this far, I believe the proverb is more relevant today than ever before; but change isn't something new. Change always happens, and always has done. Change will continue to happen; it's the only real constant. At the end of 2016 I was speaking in the Turbine Hall of what is now the Tate Modern Art Gallery in London and asked members of the audience if they had ever wondered why the building is no longer called Bankside Power Station. In fact, very few people in attendance had ever considered the detail behind the demise of the power station that led to the art gallery opening in 1993, but the story is one that neatly illustrates the point of this book.

The Middle East crisis of 1973 and 1974 rendered many UK power stations uneconomic. By the late 1970s, Bankside was used only at peak periods during the winter. Pollution from oil-fired power became unacceptable, and the increasing capability of electricity as power meant you didn't need to be so physically close to consumers, so power stations ended up being in coal-fields up in the north or nuclear stations by the coast. The entire market of being a power station diminished then disappeared within 10 years. By 1983, Bankside Power Station had shut down, along with almost every other power station in London.

In my opinion, despite the massive turbine in the center of the building, the people who ran Bankside were rather ironically building walls in the face of the winds of change, rather than windmills.

They didn't elevate; they thought they were in the business of oil-fired power. They didn't find and fix any messes; their only answer to increased pollution was to stop trading. They didn't transpose other models onto theirs; they ignored the increasing competitiveness of electricity. They didn't have, or chose not to use, all the techniques and tools that you now have, contained within these pages.

Bankside's management also didn't address the paradox of exploitation versus exploration. They maintained their rigidity, and they showed no porosity in their processes. And, it seems to me that they lacked the will, even if they had the skill, to do something about the impending doom from disruption.

I'm sure that by this point, unless you're reading the book back-to-front, you have some ideas as to what Bankside should have done. I'm sure you see that its management's ability to innovate was directly proportional to their ability to elevate. Therefore, their lack of innovation was driven by their lack of elevation. The elevation point is so critical in windmill-building. Remember, it isn't a platitude, it's a very pertinent truth—and it's practical too. Elevated organizations see the winds of change as a powering mechanism. They don't see risk and threat; they see opportunity. They don't see disruption as being dangerous; they see it as full of promise.

It perhaps seems like a cliché to state that today is the slowest pace of change we will ever experience. It is almost overused. The words change, disruption, perpetual evolution, and revolution are so common now that many of us suffer from change fatigue. But if you've made it this far in the book, I can only trust that as you read these final pages, you are now totally convinced that today is indeed the slowest pace of change we will ever experience, and that you also have a clear view of what you need to do about it.

I can imagine that at this point you are still trying to find ways to balance the paradox of exploitation versus exploration, and actually get on and implement all of these new things. I hope that you are exploring the best way to design and build your windmill blades; looking at the way that the purpose in your company is established; making sure that then infiltrates through the people; applying your new knowledge and insights to create the products that you bring to market; and ensuring that you have brilliant processes in place to achieve all of that. At the least, you might well be raring to go if you haven't already started.

But at this moment in time, please be assured that what I am not asking you to do is to scrap all of your existing business endeavors and start again. Above all else, I am asking you to do just two things.

The first is to accept that you have a binary choice between building a wall or a windmill. I want you to accept and then digest the consequences and implications of that reality. That's the first thing that I'm asking you to do, which should be relatively straightforward after the examples contained in the preceding pages, and the tangible evidence you see all around that exemplifies the perpetually blowing winds of change.

The second is a heartfelt plea. The second thing that I am asking you to do is to never stop trying. Never stop grasping hold of the opportunities when you see them and not letting go. Never stop doubling down on effort to move faster. Never stop questioning whether or not you are allowing enough information to pervade your thought processes. Never stop pursuing expertise and willingness in your people. Never limit your own curiosity and willingness to try something new. Because throughout life, there are people who try and there are those people who give up. I am hoping that because you're holding this book, you are someone who will not only try once, but will try again and again. It is those people who become the winners. It is those people who change the world. Those are the people who can change politics and change the fortunes of man. They can address world hunger and address world peace. Making any of those changes comes through trying, and not stopping.

So please—try.

Moving forward from today, you will be faced with a variety of the winds of change. You will experience many changes that may seem a long way off or futuristic, but instead can create powerful opportunities if you choose to respond rather than react.

Ultimately, it's about you using the winds of change as a powerful, enabling force, rather than seeing them as an enemy. I can only hope that you find the thoughts and suggestions in this book highly relevant to you; as you now know, you really don't have much time.

To those of you who are windmill builders, I'd love to see your progress. Please contact me at any time: j@ten.io

Acknowledgments

Despite having written numerous articles and blogs throughout the years, I've never found writing especially easy. Due to this, writing the book you are reading has required a significant level of assistance for which I am eternally grateful.

I'd like to thank Holly Bennion, Editorial Director at Nicholas Brealey Publishing in John Murray Press, for her constant and wholehearted belief in me and this book. Holly's positive approach and happy energy have often left me speechless and perpetually thankful. It is not an exaggeration to say this wouldn't have been possible without her.

I am exceptionally grateful to Jesper Brodin, CEO of IKEA Group, for writing the foreword. His faith in me is something I will never take for granted.

I'd like to thank Miriam Staley, CEO of the Thought Expansion Network, who has worked tirelessly on this book, enabling the content to transfer efficiently from my head into the written word. Andrew Cave, writer and journalist, has also been an enormous help in coaxing out my thoughts into the legible order you find within these pages.

The ITV newscaster Alastair Stewart OBE was extremely generous with his time. Being one of the first to read this manuscript, his opinion mattered a great deal and I thoroughly appreciate it.

I'd like to thank Stephen Fry, who was also an early reader of this text. Our penpal connection has been something that has meant a great deal to me over the years.

I'd like to thank Dave Birss for his illustrations, which have brought the concepts to life in an excellent way.

Although not featured within these pages, I'd like to thank Ruth Hatherley, CEO and Founder of the financial technology firm Moneycatcha Pty Ltd. (http://mcatcha.com), who has brilliantly applied the lessons inside this book into a game-changing company, with which I am honored to have been involved.

I'd like to thank all of those who have supported me in various stages of my life. My family and friends know who they are and how much I love them, but I'd like to put a special shout-out to my beautiful life partner, Malini, who continuously inspires me to be the best version of myself; my children, who are my pride and joy; and my parents, who have taught me so much over the years.

Finally, thanks to you. Thank you for investing in your own transformation. By even considering to read this book, you have entered a select group of individuals who are capable of using the modern fluctuations as an empowerment mechanism. A group of people who are truly powered by change.

This book is dedicated to all of you.

Citations & References

1 https://www.aei.org/publication/fortune-500-firms-in-1955-vs-2014-89-are-gone-and-were-all-better-off-because-of-that-dynamic-creative-destruction.

2 http://www.zmescience.com/research/technology/smartphone-power-compared-to-apollo-432/.

3 http://www.geekculture.com/joyoftech/joyarchives/2236.html.

4 https://www.fastcompany.com/919178/expand-your-innovation-horizons.

5 http://www.vanityfair.com/news/business/2012/08/microsoft-lost-mojo-steve-ballmer/amp.

6 http://www.pgconnectdevelop.com.

7 https://foundry.unilever.com.

8 http://www.deadline.com/2015/12/mystery-science-theater-3000-raises-funds-for-reboot-1201665886/amp/.

9 https://medium.com/electroloom-blog/thanks-and-farewell-b0c128c3043f.

10 http://uk.businessinsider.com/3d-printed-food-foodini-2016-4?r=US&IR=T.

11 http://www.independent.co.uk/life-style/gadgets-and-tech/news/3d-printed-skyscraper-worlds-first-built-uae-united-arab-emirates-cazza-crane-printing-a7629416.html%3Famp.

12 http://tradearabia.com/touch/article/CONS/275295.

13 http://www.theguardian.com/cities/2015/feb/26/3d-printed-cities-future-housing-architecture.

14 https://www.wsj.com/articles/SB10001424052748703632304575451414209658940.

15 http://www.mirror.co.uk/3am/weird-celeb-news/tupac-hologram-at-coachella-and-10-of-the-best-796719.amp.

16 https://hololens.reality.news/news/video-haptics-make-holograms-touchable-hololens-0175603/.

17 http://www.independent.co.uk/news/science/neural-dust-implant-sensor-brain-nerves-humans-machines-prosthetics-berkeley-a7170251.html%3Famp.

18 http://www.telegraph.co.uk/technology/2016/03/01/scientists-discover-how-to-download-knowledge-to-your-brain/.

19 http://www.dailymail.co.uk/sciencetech/article-3000904/Nanorobots-trial-begin-humans-Microscopic-DNA-devices-injected-leukaemia-patient-bid-destroy-abnormal-cells.html.

20 http://www.proteus.com.

21 http://www.sciencealert.com/a-new-start-up-wants-to-transfer-your-consciousness-to-an-artificial-body-so-you-can-live-forever.

22 http://www.wired.com/2015/09/balloon-spy-probe-deep-sweep/amp/.

23 http://www.guns.com/2015/08/04/father-arrested-after-shooting-drone-hovering-over-sunbathing-daughters-video/.

24 https://en.m.wikipedia.org/wiki/Cryonics.

25 https://www.calicolabs.com.

26 http://www.theguardian.com/science/2015/jan/11/-sp-live-forever-extend-life-calico-google-longevity.

27 https://www.forbes.com/sites/andrewcave/2016/07/25/a-billion-aire-with-a-vision-to-heal-the-worlds-blind/#13b4da545788.

28 http://www.eng.ox.ac.uk/about/news/new-study-shows-nearly-half-of-us-jobs-at-risk-of-computerisation.

29 http://www.theguardian.com/business/2015/nov/12/robots-threaten-low-paid-jobs-says-bank-of-england-chief-economist.

30 http://www.shellypalmer.com/2017/03/5-jobs-robots-will-take-last/amp/.

31 http://www.bbc.co.uk/news/technology-27426942.

32 http://www.bbc.com/news/technology-36376966.

33 https://hirepeter.com/.

34 http://www.rossintelligence.com.

35 The Power of Purpose by John O'Brien and Andrew Cave, page xxviii.

36 O'Brien and Cave, *The Power of Purpose*, 10.

37 https://www.wsj.com/articles/how-mark-parker-keeps-nike-in-the-lead-1446689666.

38 https://help-en-us.nike.com/app/answer/a_id/113.

39 http://ten.io/unlock-sessions/.

40 http://www.astalift.com.

41 http://quoteinvestigator.com/2015/04/30/reality/.

42 http://www.express.co.uk/life-style/cars/781946/Airbus-flying-car-design-Italdesign-future-modular-drone/amp.

43 https://www.google.com/intl/en/about/.

44 http://www.gallup.com/services/190118/engaged-workplace.aspx.
45 https://www.pwc.com/gx/en/ceo-agenda/ceosurvey/2017/gx/talent.html.

46 http://www.forbes.com/sites/johnkotter/2011/02/10/does-corporate-culture-drive-financial-performance/amp/.

47 O'Brien and Cave, *The Power of Purpose*, 43.

48 http://knowledge.wharton.upenn.edu/article/under-armours-kevin-plank-creating-the-biggest-baddest-brand-on-the-planet/.

49 https://careers.underarmour.com/mission-and-values.

50 https://www.investorsinpeople.com.

51 https://aira.org/cira/format.

52 https://www.amazon.co.uk/Risk-Science-Politics-Dan-Gardner/dp/0753515539.

53 http://www.thesun.co.uk/living/2535002/the-number-of-people-who-died-in-plane-crashes-in-2016-will-surprise-you-and-not-for-the-reason-you-think/amp/?

54 https://www.cuinsight.com/we-didnt-do-anything-wrong-but-somehow-we-lost.html.

55 http://www.recode.net/platform/amp/2017/3/19/14976110/uber-president-jeff-jones-quits.

56 http://www.eisp.org/1822/.

57 https://en.m.wikipedia.org/wiki/Cognitive_Surplus.

58 http://uk.businessinsider.com/tony-hsieh-zappos-holacracy-management-experiment-2015-5.

59 http://www.newyorker.com/business/currency/silicon-valley-has-an-empathy-vacuum/amp.

60 https://medium.com/@juliaculen/holacracy-not-safe-enough-to-try-434c748238e6.

61 http://www.recode.net/platform/amp/2017/1/4/14169348/medium-layoffs-ad-business-model-change.

62 https://www.tcsla.com/en_GB/blog/all-our-patent-are-belong-you.

Would you like your people to read this book?

If you would like to discuss how you could bring these ideas to your team, we would love to hear from you. Our titles are available at competitive discounts when purchased in bulk. Bespoke editions featuring corporate logos, customised covers or letters from company directors in the front matter can also be created in line with your special requirements.

We work closely with leading experts and organisations to bring forward-thinking ideas to a global audience. Our books are designed to help you be more successful in work and life.

For further information, or to request a catalogue, please contact:
business@johnmurrays.co.uk or
sales-US@nicholasbrealey.com (North America only)

Nicholas Brealey Publishing is an imprint of
John Murray Press.